KEYBOARD EDITION

HOW TO PLAY FROM A FAKE BOOK

Faking your own arrangements from melodies and chords

By Blake Neely

Crack the mysteries of a fake book by learning about chords, inversions, scales, left-hand patterns, and much more.

S0-BDO-820

ISBN 978-0-634-00206-9

ISBN 0-634-00206-6

HAL•LEONARD®
CORPORATION

7777 W. BLUEMOUND RD. P.O. BOX 13819 MILWAUKEE, WI 53213

Visit Hal Leonard Online at
www.halleonard.com

What's Inside This Great Book

Answers to Some Common Questions About Fake Books

Why do they call 'em "fake" books?

Don't let the name fool you — a *fake book* is a real music book, packed with hundreds of songs you know and love. Flip through one, and you'll quickly notice the big difference in a fake book: only the melody line, chord symbols, and lyrics are shown for each song. The accompaniment part of the song is left to you, the performer. You have to "fake" your own accompaniment or arrangement.

Who uses fake books?

All types of musicians use fake books, from amateurs to professionals. Singers can sing the melody line of a song without being distracted by the accompaniment part. Beginners can avoid intimidation by playing just the melody of a song. Professional pianists can use a fake book as a "road map" for a song's melody and harmony and dazzle the audience with their own improvised arrangements.

How much should you know about music to use this book?

Before diving into the pages that follow, you should know a few musical (and not-so-musical) things:

- *Basic piano- or keyboard-playing skills*
- *Reading music from the treble and bass clef staves (the bass clef staff is used to show you where to play left-hand chords and bass patterns)*
- *Reading rhythmic notation (half notes, quarter notes, triplets, etc.)*
- *Major scales and key signatures (a cheat sheet is provided at the back, just in case)*
- *Alphabet letters A through G (gosh, you don't even have to know letters H through Z!)*
- *Counting to 13 (that is, for counting the scale tones necessary for building chords)*

How will this book help you play from a fake book?

The art of faking accompaniments and arrangements comes from a solid understanding of **scales** and **chords**. This book shows you how to use these musical elements to make satisfying and entertaining accompaniments.

Once you know how to form chords, harmonies, and left-hand bass patterns from the chord symbols above the staff, you can easily "fake" your way through just about any song in a fake book.

Four specific abilities you gain from this book are:

- *Constructing chords from chord symbols*
- *Playing chords in different hand positions*
- *Creating interesting bass lines from chord symbols*
- *Applying various rhythmic styles to a song*

Where can you find fake books?

Most local music retailers carry a variety of fake books by publishers from around the world. Hal Leonard Corporation offers a huge catalog of over 50 great fake books (that's *thousands* of songs!). Check out the back page of this book for some titles and then *run* to your local music retailer for the ones you want.

Will any of this hurt?

I certainly hope not. Just don't turn the pages too quickly — paper cuts really sting!

CHAPTER 1
Playing with your left hand

So, let's get started. Fake book notation looks similar to that shown below. That is, the melody and lyrics are shown on a single treble clef staff with alphabet letters and symbols above the staff. These alphabet letters and symbols represent *chord symbols*, telling you which chord to play with the melody.

Don't panic if you also see some little grids above the staff, like those below. Just ignore them and use the alphabet letters. So you know, these fancy little line and dot pictures are called *guitar chord frames*. They tell guitar players where to put their fingers to play the chord. (Yes, even guitar players use fake books!)

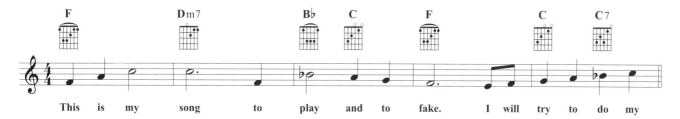

Reading from a chord line with single bass notes

Before we jump into playing chords (that'll be in Chapter 2), use the chord symbols to play single bass notes with the left hand. For example, when you see the chord symbol **C**, just play and hold the chord's *root note* **C** with your left hand until the next chord symbol comes along. Your right hand, of course, will be busy pounding out the melody.

We'll start with an easy song favorite, "Yankee Doodle." Play through the melody once by itself, then add the left-hand single notes indicated by the chord symbols. (Again, play only single root notes, not full chords.)

Yankee Doodle

American Folksong from
the Revolutionary War

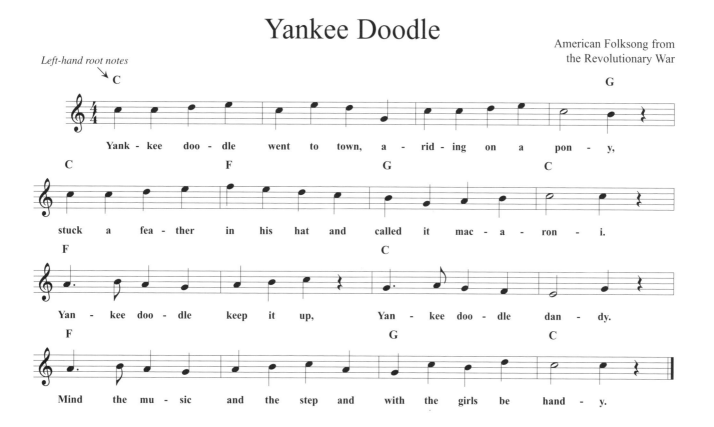

"Yankee Doodle" wasn't too difficult, was it? Try another all-time favorite that'll be stuck in your head for at least the rest of this chapter — "When The Saints Go Marching In." Again, I suggest you try the melody first before adding the left hand. (Don't get ahead of me, pal — you're still playing single root notes only with the left hand.)

When the Saints Go Marching In

Words by Kathleen E. Purivs
Music by James M. Black

Sure those two songs were easy, and sure the left-hand single bass notes won't exactly wow an audience, but you learned an important skill: *being aware of the chord symbols while playing a melody.*

Spice things up with a fifth

Any time you play two or more notes at the same time, you are playing **harmony**. The distance between any two notes is called an **interval**. An interval is measured on a scale. Got that? Read it again.

The **C major scale** below shows you each scale tone, numbered from 1 to 8. These numbers help you measure and recognize intervals.

For example, a very common interval in music is the **fifth**. It's used in tons of chords and tons of melodies. Using the C scale above, a fifth is from C (1) to G (5). (It's very easy math: just count the notes.) Other fifths are found in a similar way — D to A, E to B, F to C, G to D, and so on. Get the idea?

Try playing the fifths shown below. You should play the two notes of each fifth at the same time, using your thumb and pinky. (You can use other fingers, but I'm warning you that it may hurt.)

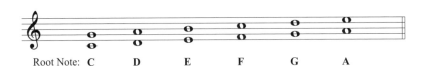

For the next song, try playing some fifths with your left-hand. That is, every chord symbol now represents the root note (or lowest note) of the fifth. Play the root with your pinky and use your thumb to add a fifth above — the fift scale tone up from the root. For example, when you see **C**, play the notes **C-G**.

Aura Lee

Words by W.W. Fosdick
Music by George R. Poulton

All of the left-hand fifths in "Aura Lee" can be located easily on the white keys, using the C major scale on page 6 as a guide. But what about black-key root notes? It's important to remember that fifths are based on the major scale of the root note. Memorizing every major scale would be very helpful but also very taxing. I have an easier tool to help you find your fifths…

The World's Easiest Fifth Finder™

Using the black keys as your guide, remember the following two helpful hints. You'll never count scale tones again to locate fifths. I guarantee it.

#1 *Fifths built on **white-key root notes** have 3 black keys in between…*

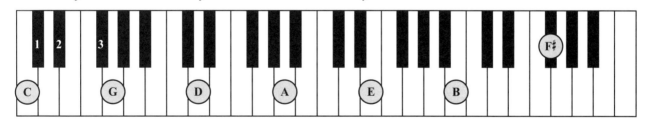

*…except for the root note **B**, whose fifth is **F♯**.*

#2 *Fifths built on **black-key root notes** have 2 black keys in between.*

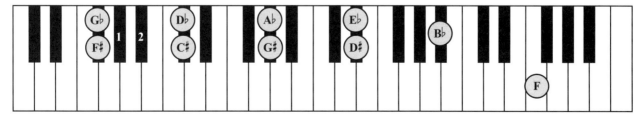

Freeze, Buster!

Notice that you can "lock" or "freeze" your left hand in position to play fifths.
This way, you can quickly find the root note with your pinky
and let your thumb just fall into place.

Let's employ some black *and* white key fifths in another crowd-pleasing classic, "Take Me Out to the Ball Game." As before, play the melody with your right hand and use the chord symbols to find the correct root-fifth intervals with your left hand.

Take Me Out to the Ball Game

Words by Jack Norworth
Music by Albert Von Tilzer

Practicing the songs in this chapter again and again will help you master the skill of reading from the chord symbol line — a critical skill in playing from a fake book.

Of course, I realize that you may tire of playing the same songs over and over. Solution? Open up a fake book and apply the same technique to just about any hit song: either single-note or root-fifth bass accompaniments. When you really have the hang of it, call some friends to come listen and cheer you on.

CHAPTER 2
Playing some major chords

A *chord* is comprised of three or more notes played at the same time. The most basic 3-note chord is called a *triad*. Which three notes do you choose? You already know two of them: the root and fifth from Chapter 1. Add one more note in between — a *major third* — and you have yourself a *major* chord. Here are some examples of major chords:

Each of the three notes in a major chord — the root, third, and fifth — comes from the major scale with the same root note, as shown in the three examples below.

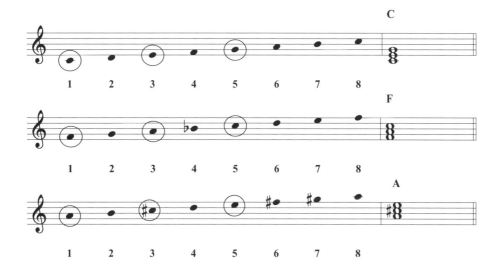

I don't expect you to know every major scale. It's certainly beneficial but not a prerequisite for learning from this book. Instead, here's another handy tool for you to use to find major thirds…

The World's Easiest Major Third Finder™

*A root note and a major third have **3 piano keys** (whether black or white) between them…*

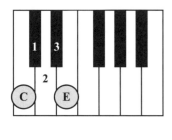
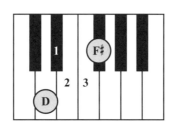
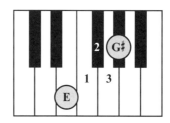

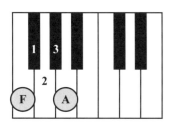
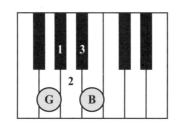
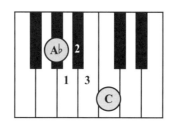

Add this note — a major third — between various roots and fifths and you have a bunch of major chords to choose from.

The shape of chords to come

Depending on the root note, a major chord can have all white keys, all black keys, or a mixture of black and white keys. There are twelve major chords, one for each separate root note.

Locate and play all twelve of these chords with your left hand. Then try playing each chord with your right hand. Who said the left hand has all the fun?

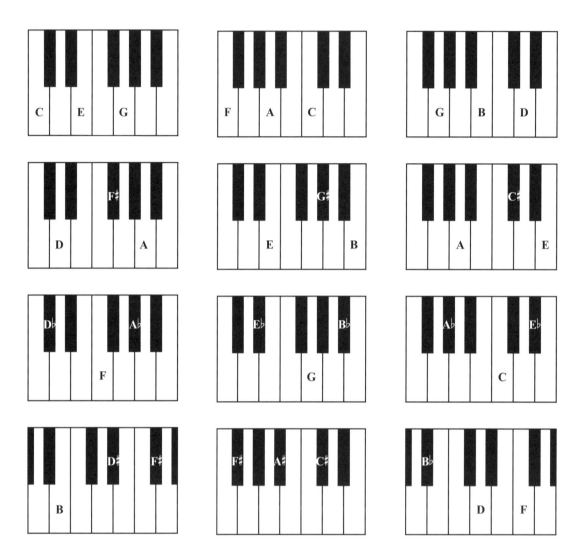

Feelings, nothing more than.

It's important to learn the "feel" of each major chord. Don't be concerned with memorizing each note in the chord right now. Just concentrate on how it feels under your fingers. I tend to think of the feel of major chords in three geometrical ways:

     1. Some major chords feel *flat* and level (**C, F, G**)

     2. Some major chords have a *triangle* shape (**D, A, E**)

     3. Some major chords have a *V* shape (**A♭, E♭, D♭**)

Try playing some major chords with both hands at the same time and notice the feel and shape of each. Use the notation on the next page as a guide but also learn the name of each chord from the corresponding chord symbol above the staff. Major chord names are easy — the same name as the root note.

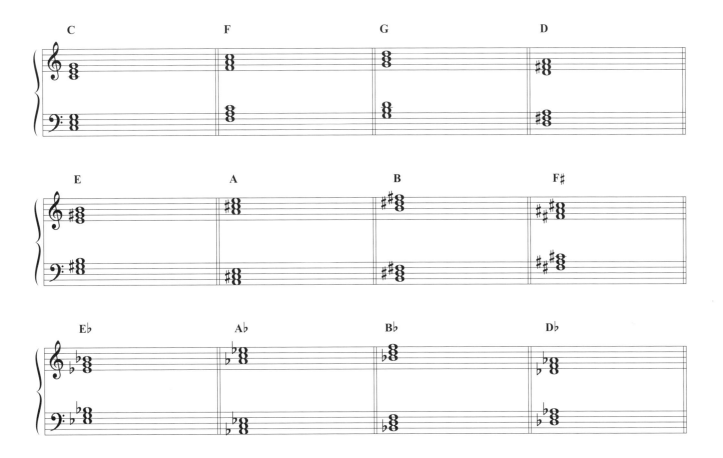

Playing Right-Hand Chords Only

To get a better feel for chords, let's play them in a well-known song. Sometimes even professionals don't feel like playing the melody, or perhaps the singer is singing the melody while the pianist fills in the chords only. That's precisely what you're about to do with the song "The Bear Went Over the Mountain."

Play chords with the right hand only while you (or a friendly bear named Yogi) sing the melody. Remember, for this one you should ignore the melody notes; just play the chords indicated by the chord symbols above the staff.

The Bear Went Over the Mountain

Folksong from the American West

Play chords only — no melody, that is — in another song, "The Yellow Rose of Texas," but this time play the root note of each chord with your left hand. For example, if you see this…

play this…

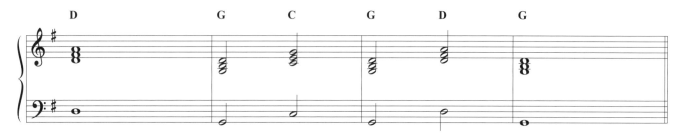

Again, don't worry about the melody notes. Just ask your friend (Yogi) to sing a little louder…if you can *bear* it! (Sorry, I admit it's a bad pun.)

The Yellow Rose of Texas

Nineteenth Century Minstrel Song

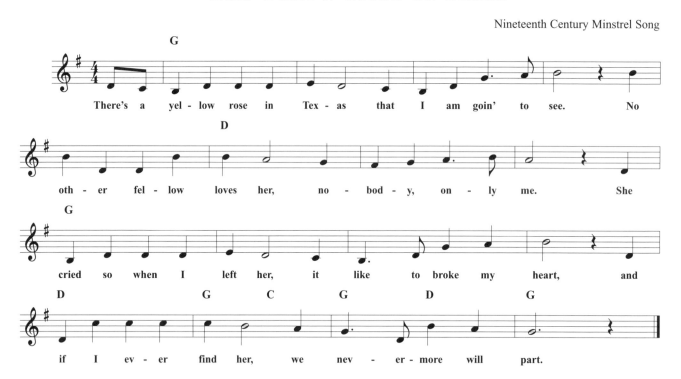

Rest your vocal chords and send your friend back to the woods for a while (you're sick of hearing him sing anyway!). It's time to play the melodies again with your right hand.

Playing Left-Hand Chords

For the next song, "Simple Gifts," play the melody with your right hand while you play the chords with your left hand. Play and hold each chord until you see the next chord change. As always, it will be advantageous to practice each hand separately, since this is your first experience with this type of playing.

Simple Gifts

Shaker Hymn

Of course, just holding chords can be rather boring and not very musical. Freshen things up a bit with a simple quarter note rhythm, as shown below in the song "Battle Hymn of the Republic." Hammer out steady quarter-note chords with the left hand. Once you're comfortable with this rhythm, add the melody with the right hand.

Battle Hymn of the Republic

Words by Julia Ward Howe
Music by William Steffe

Try a similar quarter-note rhythm but with some rests added for a bit of variety in two Stephen Foster songs. The first song, "Oh, Susannah," works well with quarter-note chords on beats 1 and 3.

Oh, Susannah

Words and Music by Stephen Foster

Use the same quarter-note/quarter-rest rhythm in "Camptown Races," but this time play the chords on beats 2 and 4 of each measure. Drummers call these the *backbeats*, but then most drummers can't read music, so don't listen to them!

Camptown Races

Words and Music by Stephen Foster

CHAPTER 3
New positions

When playing a song with lots of chord changes, your left hand is constantly moving around the keyboard to find each new chord. This can be tiring and clumsy after a while. A simple solution is to change the position of the chord.

Up to now, you've been playing your major chords in *root position*. That is, the root note of the chord — the note that names the chord — is the lowest, or bottom note, as shown below.

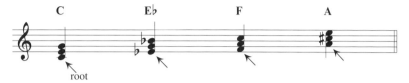

By rearranging the three notes of a chord, you can play the same harmony in a new position. That is, you can put the root note on top, or in the middle. This rearrangement of the notes is called a *chord inversion*. Here are examples of three possible positions of the **C** major chord.

As you can see, *first inversion* places the root on top; *second inversion* places the root in the middle. Play these inversions, and you'll hear that they all sound like the same **C** harmony.

It's important to practice different inversions of each major chord to get the feel and shape of each. Start with your right hand only, as notated on the treble clef staff.

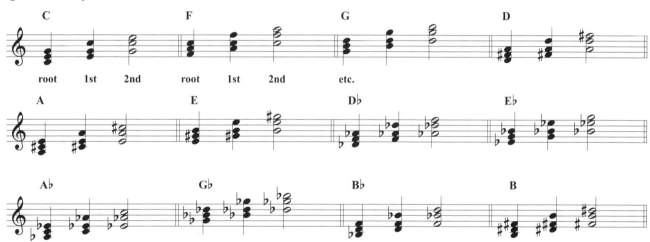

Now try the same inversions with your left hand only, as notated on the bass clef staff.

Why Learn Chord Inversions?

Here's proof: play part of the song "Red River Valley" and notice how your left hand moves around.

Red River Valley

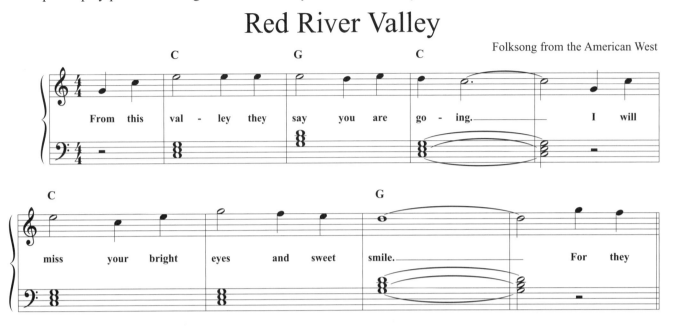

Now play the same song but with the chord inversions shown.

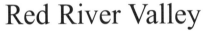

Red River Valley
(using chord inversions)

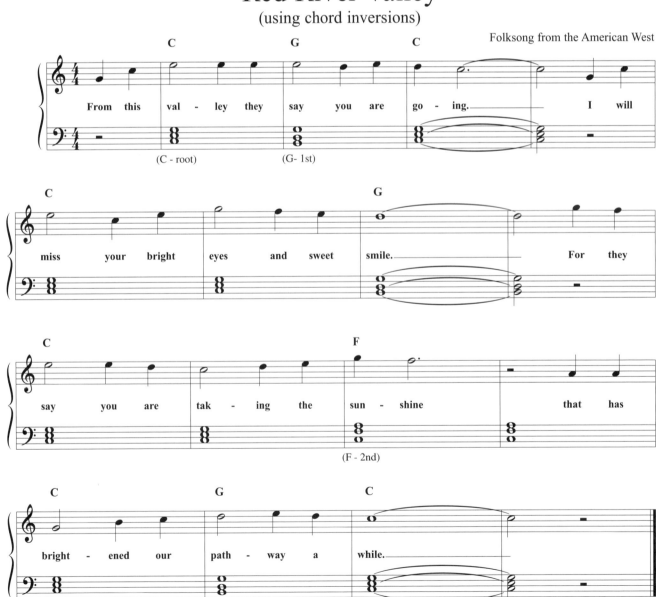

Put simply, chord inversions can make harmonic changes smoother and add variety to the music. You can even *begin* a song with an inversion, as with the first chord in the tune, "The Streets of Laredo" — an **F** in 2nd inversion.

The Streets of Laredo

American Cowboy Song

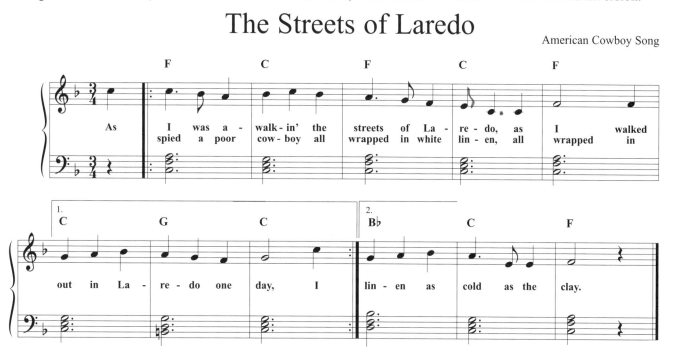

After a while, you don't even need to look at your hands — you'll feel where to move your fingers from chord to chord. That's because when you choose good chord positions and inversions, you'll find that many of the notes in one chord are very close to those in another.

Common-Tone Voicing

Choosing which chord positions to play shouldn't be an arbitrary, flip-of-the-coin decision on your part. The easiest way to move from one chord to the next is by finding a **common tone** in the two chords.

For example, look at the chords **C** and **G**. Both use the note G. The easiest way to move from **C** to **G** is to leave the G note in the same position, or *voice* — top, middle, or bottom. This requires the use of inversions, as shown below.

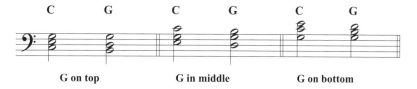

This type of chord movement is called **common-tone voicing**, because you are leaving the common tone in the same voice, or position.

An excellent way to practice this is by playing through all twelve major chords — from one to the next — but leaving each subsequent common tone in the same position.

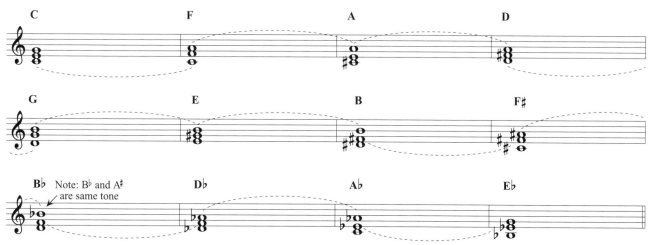

Close-tone voicing

Of course, some chords have no common tone with another. In this case, the easiest way to move between two chords with no common tone is to find positions that are *close* to each other.

For example, the chords **C** and **D** have no common tones, but the piano keys C, E, and G are close to D, F♯, and A. So, you could easily move from any position of a **C** chord to any position of a **D** chord.

Another example would be the chords **C** and **F♯**. There are no common tones in these chords, so you would find the closest position of each, as shown below.

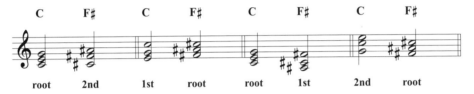

Accompany "Swing Low, Sweet Chariot" with a left-hand chord progression that utilizes common-tone voicing. Before adding the melody, it's a good idea to play through the chords first to find the common tones and feel how your left hand will move.

The chords are notated on the bass clef staff to assist you with this exercise, but you should begin to memorize each major chord's inversion for those times when the bass clef isn't shown — like in almost every fake book published!

Swing Low, Sweet Chariot

African-American Spiritual

It's all up to you.

In addition to common-tone voicing, you may find other good reasons for selecting
various chord positions, ranging from personal comfort to overall sound.

By all means, feel free to play the chord positions you like best!

After all, the primary goal of this book is to teach you how to create your *own* accompaniments,
and that includes choosing your *own* chord positions.

This is getting easier all the time. Try your hand at a few more chord changes in the song "Any Time." Again, you'll be using common-tone or close-tone voicing for your left-hand accompaniment. Once you've got the hang of it, play the song without looking at the bass clef notation. That is, try to play the chords and inversions reading from the chord symbols only.

Any Time

Words and Music by Herbert Happy Lawson

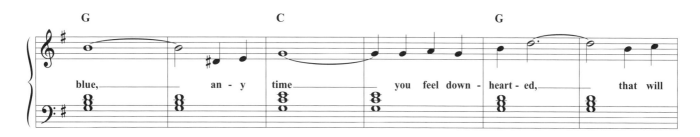

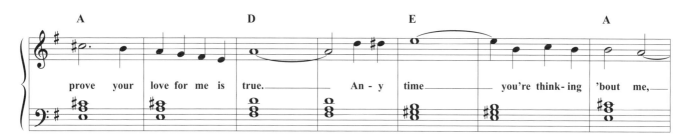

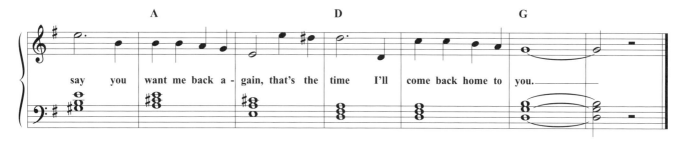

Before continuing to Chapter 4, consider playing through the songs in Chapters 2 and 3 again. It will help you begin to memorize the major chords and their inversions. Then, as you learn new chords, you won't have to spend much brain power on these old major chords.

CHAPTER 4
Introducing minor chords

If you've learned your major chords well, playing minor chords will be a cinch. Why? Because a minor chord uses the same notes as a major chord, but with one small exception: The middle note — the major third — is lowered one piano key to the left.

The major third interval (up from the root note) is now a **minor third** interval, and so the major chord is now a **minor** chord. It's just that easy! Even easier is the chord symbol — an "m" for "minor" after the letter name.

Lowering any note one piano key to the left is termed *lowering one half step*; two piano keys apart is *one whole step*. It's important to know the terms **half step** and **whole step** — you'll use them to build various chords throughout this book.

Depending on the keys used, minor chords also have unique shapes. Notice the way a **C** major chord feels under your fingers, compared to a **C** minor chord. Similarly, feel how a **G** major compares to a **G** minor chord.

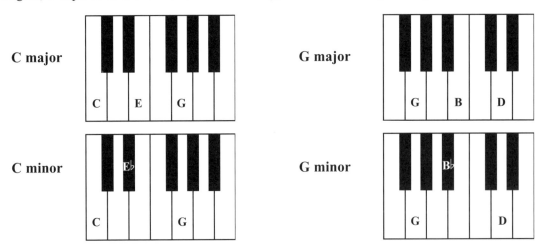

Minor chords by scale

If you prefer to think of minor chords as completely different from major chords, then create a minor chord from scratch with the aid of a minor scale. Below are some examples of minor scales and their resulting chords. (Appendix B has a list of all the minor scales, if you find this type of thing exciting.)

As you play major and minor chords with both hands, notice the subtle difference in the sound of each. Some people think of minor chords as sounding a bit "sadder" or "darker" than major chords. But it's really not about feelings (or lighting) — it's just one slightly different note in the middle.

Of course, the best exercise for learning new chords is to play them in a song. The popular English folksong "Greensleeves" is chock-full of minor chords. (Careful, it's in 6/8 meter.)

Greensleeves

Sixteenth Century English Folksong

"Hearts and Flowers" is another classic song with lots of minor chords.

Hearts and Flowers

Words by Mary D. Brine
Music by Theodore Moses Tobani

Flipping the minors around

Inversions work just the same with minor chords as they do with major chords. That is, you use the same three notes but rearrange their position — root on bottom, root in the middle, root on top.

With your left hand, play through each position of the twelve minor chords. It will help you get to know each minor chord inversion by sight and by feel.

When choosing inversions for minor *or* major chords, don't forget about that common-tone voicing thing. Refresh your memory of this great concept with the next exercise, which gives you every minor chord connected through common-tone voicing.

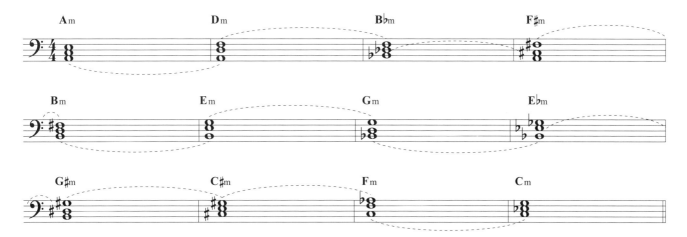

Another good exercise is to play all 12 major chords and all 12 minor chords, using common-tone voicing to move from chord to chord. You'll begin to feel how easily one chord moves into the next — whether major or minor.

When you think you have the hang of minor chord inversions, try a few of them out in the ever-popular songs "Scarborough Fair" and "Shenandoah."

Scarborough Fair

Traditional English Folksong

Shenandoah

Folksong from the American West

Left-hand options

Tired of playing the same "block chord" patterns with your left hand chords? Let's explore a few options to liven things up a bit. Each option will be given in both 4/4 and 3/4 meter…at no additional charge.

Option 1: Two-part chord

Break the chord into two parts: one note on bottom and two notes on top. This can work with a chord in root position, or an inversion. Here's how you do it. (Notice that 3/4 meter uses a slightly different rhythmic pattern.)

Option 2: Root-fifth bass

*Similar to the above, you can use a **root-fifth** bass pattern. Again, you break the chord into two parts, but this time, play the root on beat 1 and the fifth on beat 3, while playing the top two notes of the chord on beats 2 and 4. (In 3/4 meter, just forget about beat 4…well, because there is no beat 4!)*

Option 3: Arpeggio

*Perhaps you should use an **arpeggio**, or "broken chord." Instead of playing all three notes of the chord at the same time, you "break" them up and play each chord note one at a time. In 4/4, you can play all quarter notes (up and back), or two quarters and a half note (up only). In 3/4 meter, use quarter notes on each beat (up only).*

Using the song "Yankee Doodle Boy," see which of these three left-hand options works best for you. Try playing just the chords with the right hand, while you experiment with each left-hand pattern. When you're secure with these left-hand patterns, add the melody with your right hand.

Yankee Doodle Boy
(with "two-part chord" pattern)

Words and Music by George M. Cohan

(with "root-fifth bass" pattern)

(with "arpeggio" pattern)

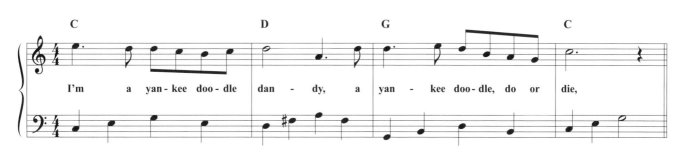

Now you're on your own. Apply each of the left-hand options to the entire song, shown below in standard fake book notation. That is, the bass clef staff isn't shown this time, so it's up to you to fake an accompaniment using the chord symbols and left-hand patterns. Good luck!

Yankee Doodle Boy

Words and Music by George M. Cohan

The next to last measure of "Yankee Doodle Boy" is an extra challenge for you. You have two chords in one measure to play with your new left-hand patterns, but each pattern you learned was for one chord per measure. No need to panic — just do this:

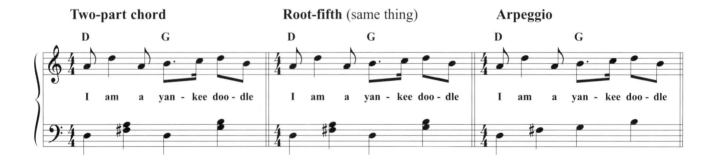

Or you may have other ideas of your own, which is fine…as long as what you play *sounds* good and doesn't send your audience clamoring for the exit.

How 'bout a song in 3/4 meter? As described on pages 24 and 25, you'll use the same left-hand patterns but with some slight modifications. This is one of Luciano Pavarotti's favorites to perform. If you play it really well, perhaps he'll ask you to accompany him at La Scala.

Come Back to Sorrento

Words and Music by Ernesto de Curtis

Try it again, maestro. Make sure you're playing the right notes for those minor chords. You'd hate to be fired by the Three Tenors.

CHAPTER 5
Don't be dominated by a dominant seventh

So you think you can handle three-note chords pretty well? That's good, because the next chord on the list uses *four* notes. The ***dominant seventh*** chord is made up of a major chord plus the ***minor seventh*** note of the scale.

As you learned with minor chords, a minor interval is formed by lowering a major interval one half-step (or one piano key to the left). So, to find the minor seventh note of the major scale, simply lower the seventh one half-step.

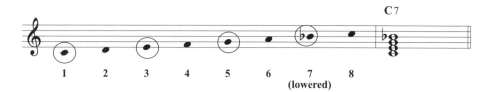

The World's Easiest Minor Seventh Finder™

There's even an easier way to find the minor seventh note. It is always a whole step (2 piano keys) lower than the root note. The minor seventh for a **C** chord is the note **B♭**, which is one whole step lower than C. How about for a **G** chord? The minor seventh is the note **F**. OK, an **F** chord? **E♭** is the minor seventh.

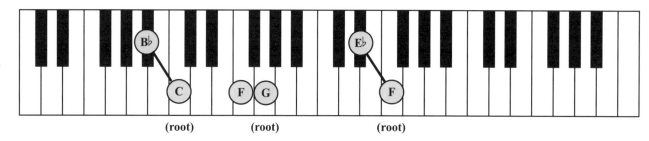

To build a dominant seventh chord, play the major chord by the same name and add the minor seventh note on top. Here are all twelve dominant seventh chords. As you can see, the chord symbol is a "7" after the chord letter name. Yes, sometimes the rules of music aren't that difficult after all.

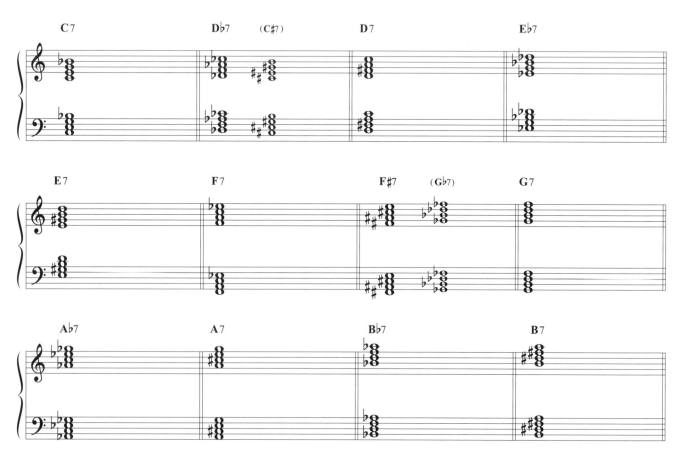

What's the difference?

Perhaps you aren't too impressed with the idea of adding a fourth note to a major chord. You have no idea why this note could make such a difference to the harmony of a song. Well, hearing is believing: play part of "Danny Boy" with only major and minor chords.

Danny Boy

Words by Frederick Edward Weatherly
Traditional Irish Melody, "Londonderry Air"

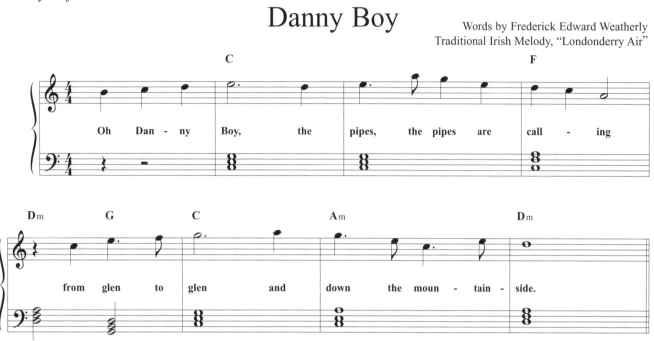

Now, play the full song but with the correct dominant seventh chords thrown in. You'll quickly hear the difference. The seventh chords add variety, and make the harmony fuller.

Danny Boy
(with dominant seventh chords)

Words by Frederick Edward Weatherly
Traditional Irish Melody, "Londonderry Air"

Drop the fifth

What? Your left hand is in pain from stretching to play so many notes? And I promised none of this would hurt. OK, here's a good solution: drop a note. But which one?

Drop the seventh? You're left with a major chord.

Drop the root? You have an entirely different chord (which you'll learn about in the next chapter).

Drop the third? Doesn't sound very good.

Drop the fifth? That's the ticket!

When you play dominant seventh chords, you can play all four notes, or choose to omit the fifth. This often makes playing seventh chords more comfortable and much easier to move from one chord to the next. As demonstrated below, it's easy to move from a **G7** (without a fifth) to a **C** (2nd inversion), an **F7** to a **B**♭, and so on.

Let's try this in a well-known Stephen Foster song. Use the bass clef staff as a guide, but notice that the first major chord (**C**) is played in 2nd inversion.

Old Folks at Home

Words and Music by Stephen Foster

And speaking of inversions...

Yes, dominant seventh chords can also be played in different positions. But since you have four notes (adding the fifth back in, of course), you have yet another possible position — ***3rd inversion***. Play each of these positions for the chords shown below.

Now that you can play seventh chords without fifths and in different positions, let's have some real fun with two song favorites, "I've Been Working on the Railroad" and "Arkansas Traveler." Again, I'm supplying the bass clef staff to show you where to position each chord. (You're welcome.)

I've Been Working on the Railroad

Folksong from the American West

32

Arkansas Traveler

Southern American Folksong

"Bouncy Chord" style

Say you're at a party, and everyone wants you to play the piano. Grab a fake book and just play the chords while the rest of the guests sing (in perfectly bad harmony, no doubt). Hey, this is a *party* — don't just play block chords. Liven things up with this "bouncy" chord style.

The left hand alternates between the root and fifth on beats 1 and 3, while the right hand plays chords on beats 2 and 4. Don't forget about those sevenths!

Try the same thing for part of "Ain't We Got Fun." The top staff shows the melody for your convenience, but you should only pay attention to the bottom two staves, playing the new "bouncy" chord-style accompaniment.

Ain't We Got Fun

Words by Gus Kahn and Raymond B. Egan
Music by Richard A. Whiting

Want to further impress those fellow party-goers? Add a ***walking bass line***. That is, when you move from one bass note to the next with your left hand, "walk" your fingers up (or down) the scale notes in between, as shown below.

Here's the same song as on the previous page but with a walking bass line. Now you're definitely the life of the party!

Ain't We Got Fun

(with walking bass line)

Words by Gus Kahn and Raymond B. Egan
Music by Richard A. Whiting

CHAPTER 6
Alterations while you wait

If you lower the major third of a major chord by one half-step, you get a minor chord. But what if you alter the *fifth* of a major or minor chord — what do you get then? (I'm sure a joke is in there somewhere.)

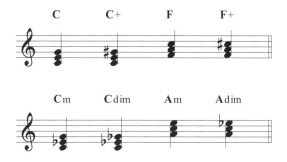

Raising the fifth of a major chord by one half-step gives you an **augmented** chord. The chord symbol is a plus sign (+) after the chord letter name. (In some fake books, you may see different symbols for this chord: **aug**, **♯5**, or **+5**.)

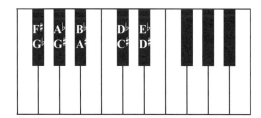

Lowering the fifth of a minor chord by one half step gives you a **diminished** chord. For this chord's symbol, you'll find either the abbreviation "dim" or a little circle that looks like a temperature sign (°) next to the chord letter name. (In some fake books, you may even see **♭5**, **-5**, **m♭5**, or **m(-5)**, although these are rare.)

Playing enharmony

No, that's not a typo — "enharmony" — it's just a play on words. As you may know, several notes (or piano keys) can be named more than one way. For example:

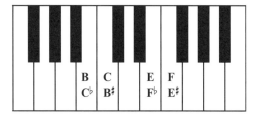

C♯ can also be called D♭, and both are played with the same black key on the piano.

F♯ can also be called G♭, G♯ can also be called A♭, etc.

When two names are used for the same note, or piano key, the notes are called **enharmonic equivalents**. Some white keys also have enharmonic equivalents:

E♯ is the same as F, and F♭ is the same as E.

B♯ is the same as C, and C♭ is the same as B.

Why am I telling you all this music theory garbage? Because when you alter the fifth of a major or minor chord, inevitably you run across some odd note names. For example, raising the fifth of an **A** major chord (E) to make an **A+** (as in *augmented* chord, not a homework grade) gives you the notes A-C♯-E♯.

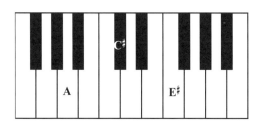

But as a pianist, you're used to thinking of that top white key as the note F, right? I thought so.

Even more awkward is the use of *double sharps* and *double flats*. I'm serious! If you lower the fifth of an **E♭m** chord (B♭) — to make an **E♭dim** chord — you get the note B♭♭ (or *B double-flat*). Ouch! Why not just call it A?

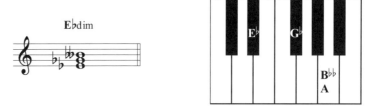

Similarly, when you raise the fifth of an **F♯** (major) chord (C♯) — to make an **F♯+** (augmented) chord — you get the note C✗ (or *C double-sharp*). Oh, come on, it's really just a D!

Less aristocratic music publishers understand your concern, confusion, and anxiety and strive to make your life less stressful by simpifying the use of such enharmonics. So, when you encounter a "different spelling" — simpler, less theoretically correct spellings — in the chords that follow, know that it's only to make things easier on you. (Thank you notes can be mailed directly to the publisher.)

Get to know your new chords

Here are the 12 major chords followed by the 12 "raised fifth" augmented chords. It's best to use the same finger to play the altered fifth of these chords. Your hand muscles will think of the chords as similar but with a slight change.

Next you have the minor chords and new diminished chords. Notice the different fingering for these two chord types.

With dominant seventh chords, it was easy enough to substitute a major chord (of the same letter name). Don't think this works so well with augmented and diminished chords. As you will hear when you play "Down By the Old Mill Stream, the sound of these new chords adds a nice element of surprise to the harmony of a song. (Not as surprising as, say, catching a shark in the old mill stream…but close.)

Down By the Old Mill Stream

Words and Music by Tell Taylor

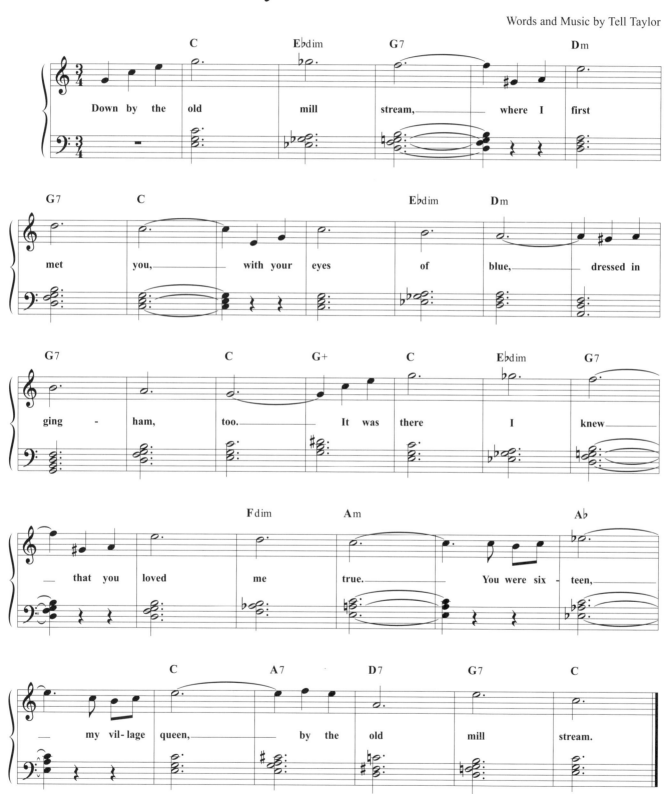

Like the sound so far? These new chords can sound pretty jazzy in the right context, as in "Give My Regards to Broadway." Try playing off-beat chords with the left hand to liven the song up.

Give My Regards to Broadway

Words and Music by George M. Cohan

Now it's your turn to play augmented and diminished chords without benefit of bass clef notation. It may be helpful to go through the song first and pencil in appropriate positions and inversions for all of the chords. Use an "R" for root position, a "1" for 1st inversion, and so on. (Or, for the artist in you, draw a tree for "root," a blue ribbon for "1st," etc.)

'Tain't Nobody's Biz-ness If I Do

Words and Music by Clarence Williams,
Porter Grainger and Graham Prince

No, I haven't forgotten.

Sure, every chord has other possible inversions, including your new augmented and diminished chords. But actually, in the case of diminished chords, inversions are rarely used. Inversions for augmented chords are more common, but I feel comfortable that you will experiment with these on your own.

Don't worry — if you *really* needed to learn these inversions, I would have given you some exercises for them.

More fun with augmented and diminished chords

Don't forget your left-hand options when it comes to playing augmented and diminished chords. You can break these chords up and play the notes individually as an arpeggio, if you tire of playing block chords.

You can also use the root-fifth bass pattern in the left hand with off-beat chords in the right hand…you know, while the pizza delivery guy sings the melody. Just remember, if it's an augmented or diminished chord, the fifth is also changed in the bass part.

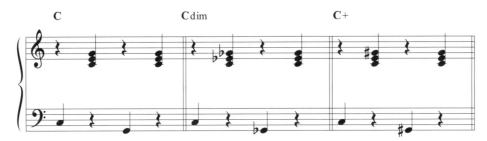

The suspense is killing me!

Another way to alter a major or minor chord is to replace the middle note (the third) with the second or fourth tone of the scale. Depending on which tone you choose, the resulting chord is called a **suspended second** or **suspended fourth**. The chord symbols for these are very clever: **sus2** or **sus4** after the chord's letter name. (A **sus4** chord is much more common and often just gets the abbreviation "sus.")

What exactly is suspended? The third (whether major or minor). Notice when you play the following chords that the suspended chord sounds unresolved, like something more should follow. When you play the the major or minor chord that follows — essentially adding the third back to the chord — you find that resolution your ear needs.

Time to try some songs that use suspended chords. The first uses a *sus4*; the second has both kinds. Have fun!

Keep the Homefires Burning

Words by Lena Guilbert Ford
Music by Ivor Novello

The Minstrel Boy

Words by Thomas Moore
Irish Folksong

Add a little suspense...

You can use a suspended chord to freshen up an otherwise stale chord progression. (It won't work with a bag of chips, though.) Even if it's not written into the chord line of a song, you can insert a suspended chord in a couple of places yourself.

Play the song "Meet Me Tonight in Dreamland" as written. Then I'll show you how and where to add some suspended chords for variety.

Meet Me Tonight in Dreamland

Words by Beth Slater Whitson
Music by Leo Friedman

The song sounds fine as is, but why not spice things up a little with some suspended chords? Here are some ideas…

As an intro...

*Because there's nothing like grabbing the audience's attention, add a short little chord intro with the use of **sus4** and **sus2** chords based on the first chord of the song. That is, since the first chord is **B♭**, play a short intro of **B♭sus4**, **B♭**, **B♭sus2**, **B♭**, then continue the song. (This is most effective with a slow song, or ballad.)*

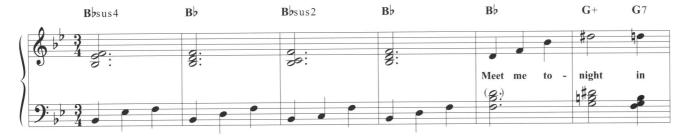

At the end of a phrase...

*As the first verse (or chorus) comes to an end, make the last chord of the phrase into a **sus4** or **sus2** chord for the first two beats, followed by the original chord written. For example, the first phrase of lyrics ends with two measures of an **F7** chord. Change this to one measure of **Fsus4** and one measure of **F** (or **F7**). This will add some harmonic variety and lead into the next musical phrase nicely.*

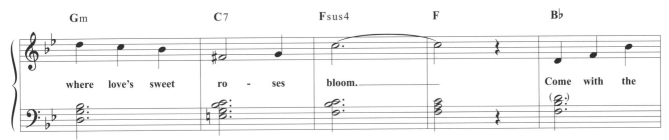

As an "outro"...

*To make the ending a bit snappier, insert a measure of suspended chords based on the last chord of the song. That is, play the last chord (**B♭**) and insert a measure of **B♭ sus** chords before playing the final **B♭** chord again. (Of course, if the audience wants more, just repeat the song from the beginning.)*

Now play the entire song, "Meet Me Tonight in Dreamland," again with these ideas. You might want to pencil in the "new" suspended chords in the chord line, so you'll know exactly where you want to play them.

Sharpen your pencil, sharpen your skills.

Speaking of scribbling down chords, it's a good idea to keep a pencil handy when you play from fake books. When creativity strikes, jot down your ideas right on the music, whether it's an added chord, a bass line pattern, or a recipe from the restaurant chef.

Hey, you bought the fake book — you can do with it whatever you want.

CHAPTER 7
When your right hand gets bored

Perhaps you're tired of playing a plain Jane, single-note melody with your right hand. Perhaps you'd like some variety. Well, there are quite a few things you can do.

For starters, you can add harmony to the right hand. Why? There are several possible reasons:

1. *You're aren't able to play the chords with your left hand because it's busy playing a single-note bass line.*

2. *You're playing arpeggios with your left hand but still want the full chords to sound.*

3. *You really want to emphasize the chords.*

Any of these are fine reasons to add harmony to the right hand melody. And you can do this several ways.

Add chord notes to the melody

Most of the notes in a melody are the same ones found in the chords of the song. So, to add harmony to the right hand, just add in the missing notes from the chord. Using a song like "Kum-bah-yah," for example, you can see how comfortably these additional chord notes fit under the melody notes you're playing.

Of course, chords like that (on every melody note) can sound pretty bad after a while, especially in a quiet song beside a campfire. Instead, hold the added chord notes with two lower fingers while you play the melody notes with the upper fingers. (Your friend can toast the marshmallows for you while you're busy playing.)

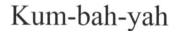

Kum-bah-yah

African-American Slave Song

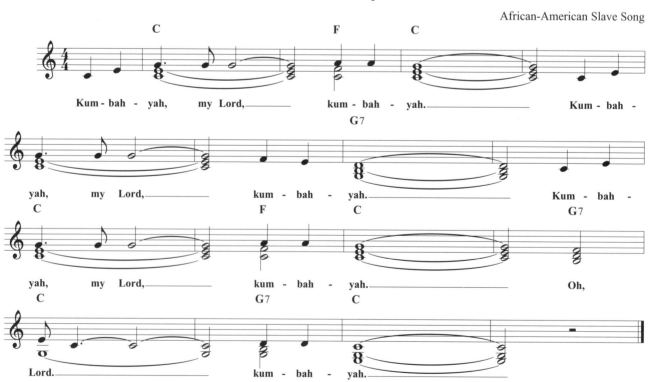

Off-beat harmony

Another great right-hand harmony technique is to play the extra chord notes on the off-beats, or during one long held melody note.

Try this in the song "She'll Be Comin' 'Round the Mountain." It's tricky to get the hang of this bouncy feel, but once you do, you'll have a hard time stopping. When you're really good at it, try adding the single-note bass line.

She'll Be Comin' 'Round the Mountain

Folksong from the American West

What's that great bass line?

Did you skip Chapter 5? Shame on you. It's nothing more than a *walking bass line*, using the root and fifth of each chord and sometimes walking up (or down) the scale notes in between. Page 34 explains how this works. Don't let me catch you skipping pages again!

Vary the rhythm of the melody

Adding harmony isn't the only way to liven up the right hand. If you're bored with the melody but don't feel like adding additional chord notes, just vary the rhythm. (Think twice before doing this if the composer is a member of the audience!)

Here are some examples of rhythmic variations, using the melody "Michael, Row the Boat Ashore."

Original melody

Although I wasn't there when the composer wrote it, I'm assuming the original melody goes like this (since this is how it's always published):

Change the bland quarter notes

Whenever you have two quarter notes in a row, change them to an eighth note/dotted quarter note rhythm, which sounds sort of "jazzy."

Anticipate and syncopate the beat

*Take this a bit further by playing some of the melody notes early. Anticipate beats 1 and 3 by starting the note on the **upbeats** ("ands") of 4 and 2, as shown below. It helps to count the beat out loud as "1 and, 2 and," etc.*

Using these ideas, add your own rhythmic variations to the entire song. A more rhythmic left-hand chord pattern will also keep things hopping. Experiment with various rhythms, much like a jazz singer would improvise the melody.

Michael, Row the Boat Ashore

Traditional American Folksong

Try your rhythmic variations with another fun song that seems to cry out for improvisation…

St. James Infirmary

Words and Music by Joe Primrose

When you're comfortable with improvising a cool right-hand rhythm, add the chords in the left hand. As the melody becomes more syncopated, it's nice to keep the left hand "steady" with quarter-note or half-note chords.

But, then again, sometimes it's fun to emphasize the syncopation with both hands, as shown below.

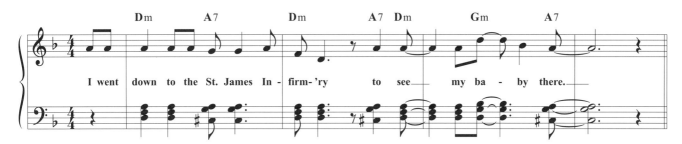

Any darn way you choose to do it, adding rhythmic and harmonic variety to a right-hand melody is a fun and easy way to make fake book music more exciting (and danceable).

CHAPTER 8
More seventh chords

So, you feel quite proficient adding the minor seventh note to major chords to make dominant seventh chords, do you? Good, because that lovely note can also be added to lots of other chord types.

Remember, the easy way to find the minor seventh is to locate the note that is two piano keys (or one whole step) lower than the chord's root note.

Oh, come on, admit it — you already experimented with adding that note to other three-note chords, didn't you? Well, if you didn't yet, now's the time. You can add a minor seventh to minor chords, augmented chords, diminished chords, even suspended chords. And it's that easy — just add it!

The names have been changed to protect the innocent

Notice that the names are slightly different when the seventh is added to an augmented or diminished chord. The resulting chord symbol tells you exactly which notes to play. For example, a **C7♯5** tells you to play a **C7** chord and *raise the fifth*, which is an augmented chord with the minor seventh added.

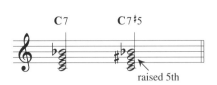

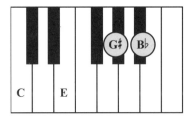

Similarly, a **Cm7♭5** tells you to play a **Cm7** chord and *lower the fifth*, which is actually a **Cdim** chord with a minor seventh note added.

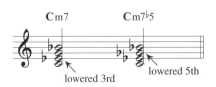

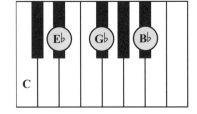

Why does it have to be so complicated?

CAUTION: Another chord symbol looks like it means "diminished chord with minor seventh added," but it doesn't mean that at all. It's an entirely different chord.

You may have seen the chord symbol **Cdim7**. Yes, it does mean *diminished seventh*, but it does not mean to add a minor seventh to a diminished chord. Instead, it means to "diminish" (or lower) the minor seventh note.

Patience, my friend. You'll learn all about this confusing chord symbol in the next chapter.

Before we try some songs, compare the three-note versions of your various chord types with the new "7th sound." Just as it did with major chords, the minor seventh note adds even more harmonic variety to the chords you already know and love.

Minor seventh chords

The next song has some good examples of your new minor seventh chord.

My Country 'Tis of Thee

Words by Samuel Francis Smith
Melody "God Save the King"

Jerome Kern was no stranger to minor seventh chords, as you'll hear in the refrain from "They Didn't Believe Me." Notice how common-tone voicing helps you move easily between the chords of this song.

They Didn't Believe Me

Words by Michael E. Rourke
Music by Jerome Kern

Add a seventh to your augmented and diminished chords

Since minor seventh chords aren't too challenging for you, try adding the minor seventh note to your augmented and diminished chords in three great songs. Be on the lookout for those chord symbols with ♯5 or ♭5 in them.

Frankie and Johnny

Nineteenth Century American Folksong

Royal Garden Blues

Words and Music by Clarence Williams
and Spencer Williams

Beale Street Blues

Words and Music by W.C. Handy

Suspended seventh chords

Just like the others, all you have to do for this new chord is play a *sus4* or *sus2* chord and then add the minor seventh note to the mix. Check it out for yourself in a verse from the song "Shall We Gather at the River?"

Shall We Gather at the River?

Words and Music by Robert Lowry

CHAPTER 9
Even more seventh chords

I realize we've shown some favoritism to the minor seventh note of the scale, adding it to countless numbers of major, minor, and other chord types. Sure, the minor seventh is (arguably) the most common tone to add to a three-note chord, but it ain't the only one.

Look at the *C major scale* again, and recall that the seventh note up the scale is actually **B natural**.

This seventh is a perfectly good note, too, and can be added to major and minor chords to form a new chord called a *major seventh* chord. The name is derived from the fact that the new added note is a *major seventh* interval from the chord's root note. Below are some examples of major seventh chords.

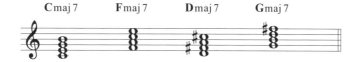

Added to a **C** major chord, you get the chord symbol **Cmaj7**. You may also see **CM7**, which means the exact same thing. (If you're playing overseas, you may even see **CΔ7**. Again, same chord but strange chord symbol.) Added to a minor chord, the *maj7* suffix is placed in parentheses (to avoid a clash between the two "m's"), as **Cm(maj7)**.

Playing sevenths in a major way

Try making some major sevenths from your 12 major and 12 minor chords.

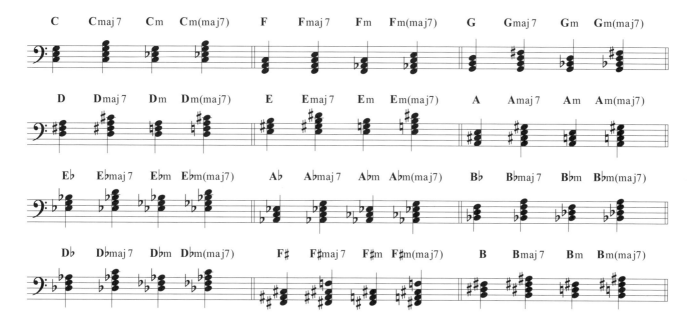

An otherwise dull melody, like "Jingle Bells," morphs into a jazzy little number with the help of your new major seventh chords. Pay attention to the sound of these new chords and how they affect the song's harmony. (Of course, you'll also find some of your other seventh chords in this example.)

Jingle Bells

Words and Music by J.S. Pierpont

Here's another good song with lots of opportunity to practice your major sevenths. But this time you don't have the bass clef — you're on your own. Hey, after a couple of runs through, you too will beg the question…

How Can I Keep From Singing?

American Folk Hymn

Lowering the seventh again

In the previous chapter, you learned about adding a minor seventh to a diminished chord (or a **7♭5** chord). This is not the same, however, as a *diminished seventh* chord. Close, but no cigar.

A diminished seventh chord is a diminished chord with a ***diminished seventh*** note. (Perhaps it should be called a ***diminished-diminished seventh*** chord, but it's not.) In other words, you lower the seventh note of the scale again, as shown below with other seventh chords you know. (Enharmonics are usually simplified to avoid the double-flat thing.)

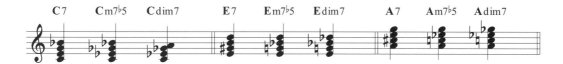

You can think of this note as a *major seventh lowered one whole step*, or a *minor seventh lowered one half step*. Either way, this note is **3** piano keys (a minor third) lower than the chord's root note.

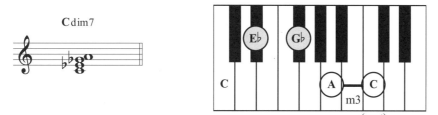

Another easy way to think of this chord is how you build it: *by stacking minor thirds on top of one another*. Notice that there are always **2** piano keys between each note in a diminished seventh chord.

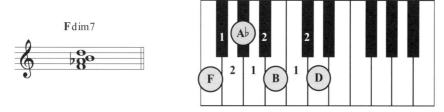

However you care to think of them, try playing all 12 diminished seventh chords. Notice that you can use the exact fingerings for these as you do for a dominant or major seventh.

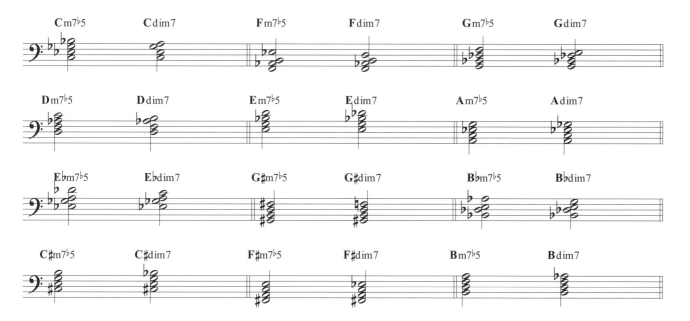

Many popular songs employ these diminished seventh chords (far more than I can include in this one book). Here are a couple for your musical delight — an excerpt from the windy city's toddlin' anthem and a song about smooching. Of course, don't forget all the other chord types you've learned. They'll inevitably toddle in from time to time along with your new diminished sevenths.

Chicago (That Toddlin' Town)

Words and Music by Fred Fisher

I Wonder Who's Kissing Her Now

Words by Will M. Hough and Frank R. Adams
Music by Joe E. Howard and Harold Orlob

I won't tell anybody that you cheated.

For whatever reason, you may not always feel like playing the diminished seventh note of a **_dim7_** chord. That's OK — just reduce the **_dim7_** chord to a plain three-note diminished chord (**_dim_**).

It won't have quite the same harmonic *oomph*, but if you keep the song lively, your audience probably won't be able to tell what was missing.

CHAPTER 10
Chords with additives...accept no substitutes

Yes, seventh chords are indeed "chords with additives," or three-note chords with an added note. But you wanted a catchy title for this chapter, right? So, same idea as before: you're going to add other scale notes to your major and minor chords to make completely new and even more exciting chords.

Take a look at our trusty *C major scale* again. The scale tones you should know for this chapter are the **2nd** and **6th**.

There's nothing tricky about these notes. In fact, they're both very easy to find.

*A **second** is always one whole step (or 2 piano keys) above the chord's root.*

*A **sixth** is always one whole step (or 2 piano keys) above the chord's fifth.*

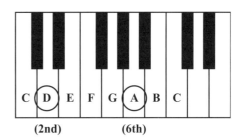

Now that you know where these two notes are, let's put the cart before the horse (or count backwards) and start with the sixth. (Please don't ask why — I have no good reason for it.)

Sixth sense about harmony

Adding the sixth to a chord creates — brace yourself! — an ***added sixth*** chord. (Yes, it's that easy.) Play any major or any minor chord and add the sixth on top. The chord symbol is — you're gonna love this! — a "6" after the chord letter name for major (**C6**) or after the letter name and "m" (**Cm6**) for minor.

Play all twelve major and minor chords with added sixths.

When you think you have these chords under your fingers well enough, see how they sound in a song. Folk tunes like "All God's Children Got Shoes" and "Bury Me Not on the Lone Prairie" let you hear how nicely these chords can enhance a song's overall harmony.

All God's Children Got Shoes

African-American Spiritual

Bury Me Not on the Lone Prairie

Words based on the poem "The Ocean Burial"
by Rev. Edwin H. Chapin
Music by Ossian N. Dodge

If you aren't convinced that it's worth adding the sixth to a chord, I urge you to play the songs again but without any sixth chords. That is, if you see **Dm6**, just play a **Dm** chord. I'm sure you'll soon agree that the sixth is a welcome addition to the chord. (Hey, that's probably why the composer wrote it that way!)

Make up your mind — second or ninth?

For your next chord with attitude…er, additive…you add the second note of the scale to any major or minor chord. Doing so, you get — this one's a doozy! — an ***added second*** chord. The chord symbol for this new chord actually tells you exactly what to do: **add2**. (Some fake books may also use just a "2" (**C2**), but this is rare.)

You may also see the chord symbol **C(add9)**. *What?!*

OK, before I explain this, let's try a little experiment: If the ***C major scale*** had nine notes, what note would the ninth one be? (This is not a riddle.)

I don't mean to rattle your foundations; the major scale, indeed, has only eight notes. But when it comes to building chords, musicians often refer to notes *beyond* the scale. (Probably so people will think they can count higher than 8.)

By doing so, as you can see below, the *ninth* note is the same as the *second* (except that it's one octave higher). For this reason, an ***added second*** chord is often called an ***added ninth*** chord. (Again, to prove to people that these musicians know their math!)

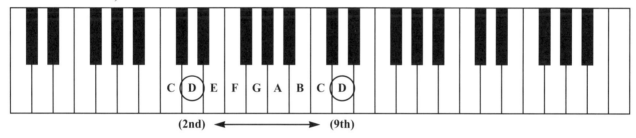

Take a crack at playing these multi-named, note-added chords. The exercise below gives you all 12 major and minor chords, followed by their respective added second/added ninth versions.

It just so happens that the melody note is sometimes the second or ninth needed for the added second/added ninth chord. When this is the case, you can just play an appropriate three-note major or minor chord below it and let the melody note provide the "added" harmony.

Do this in the songs "Way Down Yonder in New Orleans" and "Old Joe Clark." I've circled the melody notes that make the added second (or ninth) harmony. You'll notice that this note is left out of the chord on the bass clef staff. Of course, you can add it back in, if you really want to emphasize that note.

'Way Down Yonder in New Orleans

Old Joe Clark

Folksong from Tennessee

Don't drop the fifth or third!

You may be thinking back to those times (from previous songs and chapters) when you dropped the fifth from your seventh chords and inversions. Not with these guys, I implore you! For that matter, don't drop the third either. Here's why:

Drop the fifth of an added sixth chord?
You have a minor chord, first inversion. Good chord, wrong harmony.

Drop the fifth of an added second chord?
You get a cluster of three very close notes. (Yuck!)

Drop the third of an added second chord?
You now have a **sus2** chord.

One more thing: I shouldn't have to tell you (but I will) that if you drop the third of a minor sixth chord, you no longer have a minor chord at all (since the third makes a minor chord minor).

Every chord should have a voice

In earlier chapters (and even in this one), you learned to add harmony to the right hand. But you were usually adding all of the chord notes to the melody, while the left hand played a walking bass line, or something. Sometimes, though, it is quite acceptable to split up the notes of a chord and play some of them with the left hand and some with the right hand, like this…

Neither hand is playing enough notes to constitute a whole chord, but together the hands are playing a very nice-sounding harmony.

This type of chord playing is called ***chord voicing***. You decide which position (or voice) to play each note of a chord. Plus, spreading the voices out gives the chord a richer, fuller sound.

When should you use chord voicing? There are several appropriate times:

1. *If you want to play chords only while the party guests (or I.R.S. auditors) sing the melody, chord voicing provides a richer harmony.*

Words by E.P. Christy
Popular Foksong from the mid-1800s

2. *If you don't want to **double** any notes in the melody. That is, if the melody note is an E, you can leave out the E in a left-hand **C7** chord.*

3. *If you want to add harmony to a right-hand melody, but you don't want to add whole chords.*

Chords with four notes are easiest to voice, because you can put two notes in each hand. This will work well with all seventh chords (dominant, major, diminished, etc.), added sixths, and added seconds. For the song "Carolina in the Morning," you might try voicings similar to the following:

Carolina in the Morning

Words by Gus Kahn
Music by Walter Donaldson

Even Beethoven ended with a ninth...

(Well, ninth *symphony*, that is.) Want to end your songs the way multi-platinum pop artists do? Yep, I thought so. If you're playing a nice slow ballad, make the last chord an **add9**. In other words, add the ninth note of the scale to whatever chord is at the end.

Anyone listening will have to look twice to make sure you're not Elton John or some other superstar.

CHAPTER 11
Slash chords

You may think this is an introduction to scary chords from teen horror movies. Well, it's not — sorry to disappoint. Rather, **slash chords** are a type of chord notation used by composers and arrangers to tell you, the player, what bass note to use under a particular harmony.

But before getting into the technical aspect of these new chord symbols, just have a look at some of them:

Don't confuse the meaning of these slash chord symbols. The symbol **C/E** does not mean to play the chords **C** major and **E** major at the same time. (That would sound rather funky.) It means to play a **C** major chord *over* a bass note E.

You may even see slash chord symbols written exactly like that, as shown below:

Adding a little bass

The easiest way to acommodate this type of chord symbol is to play the chord with your right hand and the specified bass note with your left, as in the example below.

But how 'bout when you're busy playing the melody with your right hand and chords with your left hand. How do you incorporate the requested bass note? Using an excerpt from the song "The Bowery," look at some of your options for tackling such dilemmas.

Use an appropriate inversion

Remember, when you use chord inversions, you are putting a note other than the root on bottom. If the slash chord is a **G7/D**, *for example, you can simply play a* **G7** *chord in second inversion.*

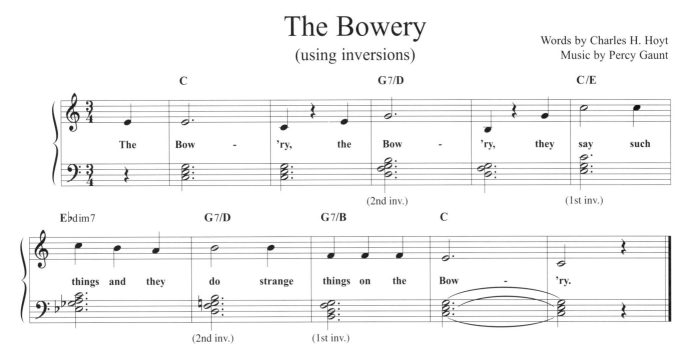

Use two-hand chord voicings

Just as you did in the previous chapter, you can add chord notes to the right-hand melody and play the remaining chord notes with your left hand…with the desired bass note on bottom, of course.

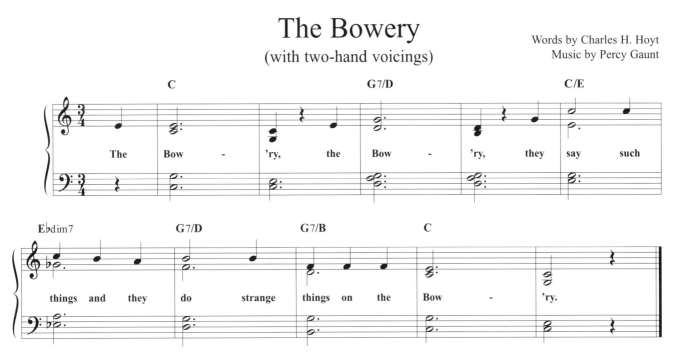

68

Use a left-hand chord option

You haven't forgotten the two-part "broken chord" option, have you? If the slash chord is **G7/D**, *just break it up and play a* D *bass note on beat 1 of the measure, followed by a* **G7** *chord (or parts of it) on the following beats.*

The Bowery
(using two-part chords)

Words by Charles H. Hoyt
Music by Percy Gaunt

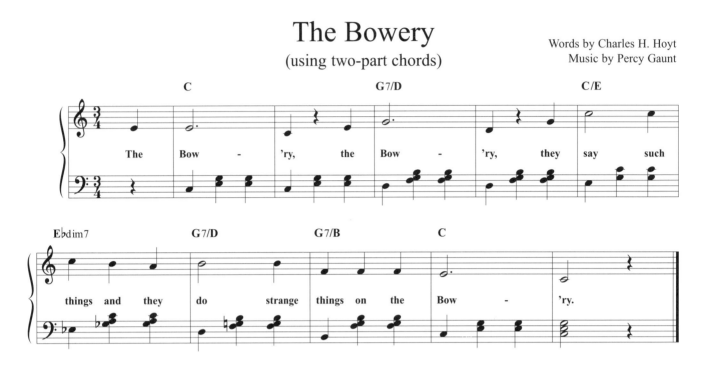

What's the point?

Slash chords specify how the bass line of a song should sound. Further, it tells you how to voice the harmony. And when it comes to faking your own arrangements, any help you can get should be a welcome gift.

To illustrate how important slash chords can be to a song's harmony, play the opening bars from the song "Home on the Range." As you can see, there are no slash chords in this example. Bear with me, pardner — I'm illustrating a point.

(By the way, play each chord in root position for this example.)

Home on the Range
(without slash chords)

Words and Music by
Dr. Brewster Higley
and Daniel E. Kelley

Now try the same song again, but this time with the addition of slash chords. Notice how the use of these bass notes creates a sort of walking, or descending, bass line. This adds a nice harmonic effect to an otherwise plain melody. (Not to imply, however, that "Home on the Range" is a dull melody, Dr. Higley and Mr. Kelley!)

Home on the Range

(with slash chords)

Words and Music by
Dr. Brewster Higley
and Daniel E. Kelley

Accompanist, P.I. (Detective for Hire)

Slash chords won't always create an evenly-spaced descending, or ascending, bass line. Heck, some bass lines jump all over the keyboard. But you can still figure out what harmony is intended with a little bit of detective work.

When you encounter a song with slash chords, forget the melody the first time through and just play single bass notes under right-hand chords. This way, you can hear the harmony and bass line without the distraction of the melody.

Knowing the correct sound of the harmony will help you fake better accompaniments.

Here's another song with slash chords. I've notated a broken chord accompaniment for you, but feel free to make up something new while reading from the chord line. (Hey, that's the fake book way!)

My Melancholy Baby

Words George A. Norton
Music by Ernie Burnett

Slow and bluesy (play ♫ as ♩♪)

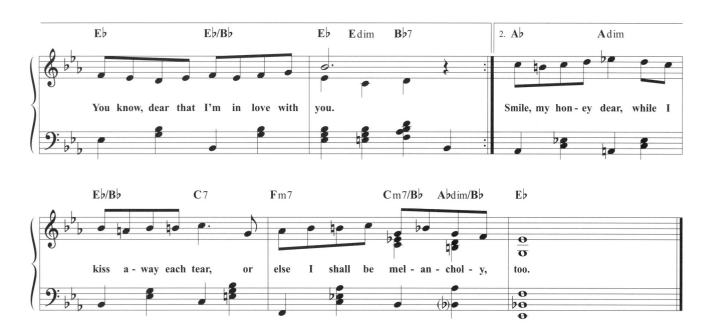

Hey, that note ain't part of the chord?!

Sometimes you'll see a slash chord with a bass note that isn't even part of the original chord. For example, **F/G** is a perfectly good slash chord, but the note G is not (as you well know) part of an **F** major chord. Don't worry too much about the theoretical implications — just play it!

Using the left-hand options at your disposal, you might choose to play the following musical line…

…like this (with broken chords):

…or like this (with two-hand chord voicing):

Or even some other cool way you've discovered.

Of course, you might choose to ignore the slash chord. Yes, it's your prerogative. Sure, you won't have to worry about how to voice the chord. Indeed, it's a lot simpler that way. But who wants to listen to a lazy pianist?

Now try a popular song that employs slash chords with bass notes from "outside" the original chord. I would advise playing the chords in the right hand and bass notes in the left the first time through. Then, after you know how the harmony should sound, add the melody and some two-part broken chords. Good luck!

I'm Called Little Buttercup
from H.M.S. PINAFORE

Words by W. S. Gilbert
Music by Arthur Sullivan

CHAPTER 12
Extending your chordal horizons

As you learned in the Chapter 10, chords can be made with notes from an "extended" scale, or one that keeps on going past the octave note (number 8). This is how you get the ninth for an **add9** chord. And it's also how you'll get the notes you need for the new chords in this chapter.

Suppose we kept counting scale notes even past the ninth. Oh, what the heck — it may be an unlucky number, but let's make the scale 13 notes long. This would result in the following notes:

Circled are scale tones 9, 11, and 13 — not because they're good lottery picks — because they are the notes necessary for building some new chords called (get this!): *ninths*, *elevenths*, and *thirteenths*. And can you guess what the chord symbols are for these humdingers? **C9, C11, C13**. No kidding!

Here are examples of these new chord types. See if you can detect what's happening in each chord. If not, I'll explain all about them in the next few sections.

All kinds of ninths

You may be wondering how a *ninth* chord is different from an *added ninth* chord. They both "add" the same note from outside the scale. But here's the big difference: the seventh note is also part of a ninth chord. In fact, the *type* of seventh note determines the *type* of ninth chord. (That seventh is one powerful dude, huh?)

The chord symbol tells you which seventh note to use to create the correct type of ninth chord. Hey, the chord symbol practically spells out *all* the notes for you. Take a look…

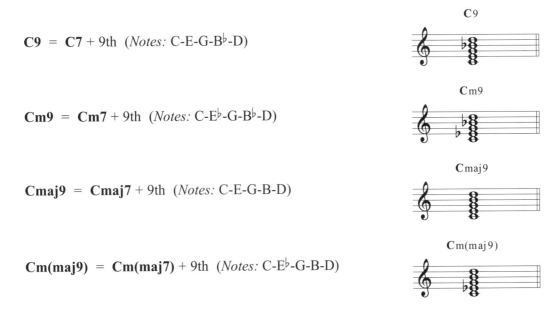

C9 = **C7** + 9th (*Notes:* C-E-G-B♭-D)

Cm9 = **Cm7** + 9th (*Notes:* C-E♭-G-B♭-D)

Cmaj9 = **Cmaj7** + 9th (*Notes:* C-E-G-B-D)

Cm(maj9) = **Cm(maj7)** + 9th (*Notes:* C-E♭-G-B-D)

It's too big for one hand!

Unless your name is Rachmaninoff, Liberace, or Plastic Man, it's quite difficult to stretch all five fingers on one hand to grab all five notes in these big new chords. That's precisely why you learned the concept of *chord voicing* in the previous chapter. (And you thought it was just a space-filler?)

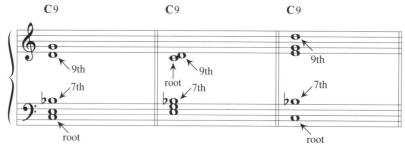

To play ninth chords well (and, later, 11ths and 13ths), you should use two-hand chord voicings. Of course, in some cases, you may find that the melody note is the "ninth," in which case you can just play an appropriate seventh chord below it with your left hand, as shown below.

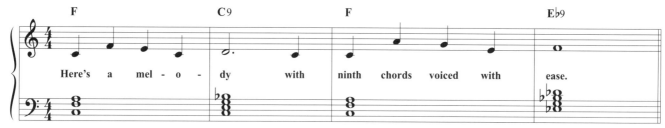

Try playing some of the different types of ninth chords. Each are voiced the same way in this exercise..

More hot tips on how to cheat!

You can reduce the ninth chord to a smaller one with similar tones. A **C9** has the notes C-E-G-B♭-D. Pick any four of these notes and you can build a **C7**, **Em7♭5**, **Gm6**, or a **Cadd9** to play instead of the two-handed ninth chord.

Remember what Mom always said: if you can't play (it) nice, don't play (it) at all.

Elevenths and thirteenths

Going on up the *C major scale* again, reacquaint yourself with the 11th and 13th notes. You'll notice that these are the same notes (but one octave higher) as the 4th and 6th, respectively.

If you forget this, just remember the number "7." You can subtract 7 from any extended scale tone to find it's lower counterpart, as shown below. (But please don't get too bogged down with these algebraic equations — 13 is as high as you'll have to count in this book.)

You can't just add an 11th or 13th to a major chord, though. Nope. Just like the ninth chords you learned, there are other important scale tones that must be present in the chord to make a proper eleventh or thirteenth chord harmony. And can you guess which scale tones they are? Why, yes, it's the teacher's pet "7" and his partner in crime "9."

Play the following chords and pay attention to the subtle differences in sound, created by the addition or subtraction of the all-important 7th and 9th.

And you thought ninths were big!

Since you don't have six fingers on each hand, you'll have to choose an option to play these big new chords:

1. *Voice the chord in both hands.*

2. *Reduce the eleventh or thirteenth to a smaller chord with similar tones.*

3. *Grow a third arm.*

It's your choice…well, the third option is sort of nature's choice.

Playing with the big kids

Although these big chords aren't as common as ones from previous chapters, composers tend to throw them in every now and then to make their songs a little hipper. (Gospel music is especially good at employing these big chords.) Or these chords can be used to add a new harmony to a popular song, as shown in "America, the Beautiful."

With a little help from all of your chords (big and small), you can have a completely new harmonic treatment of a well-known tune. A richer harmony adds emotion and musical resonance to a meaningful song such as this one.

America, the Beautiful

Words by Katerine Lee Bates
Music by Samuel A. Ward

This next song's big chords are already voiced across two hands for you. Just don't get used to this kind of friendly help. When it comes to real fake book playing, there is no such thing as friendly accompaniment help.

April Showers

Words by B.G. DeSylva
Music by Louis Silvers

CHAPTER 13
Make your own kind of music

When you know how to make great chords, you're well on your way to making great music. But there's one more thing you should know to be adept at fake book playing: *creating the overall arrangement.*

This final chapter will give you more ideas for dressing up the melody and making it sound like your own. Then you'll go step-by-step and see how to take any song from any fake book and apply the wonderful stuff you've learned to "fake" a great accompaniment.

Handy tools to keep around the house

If you ever come across a chord symbol that looks foreign to you — and, believe me, there are plenty out there in the world of music — there are a couple of tools you can use to build just about any chord from just about any chord symbol.

Do what it says

The chord symbol says **C♯7♭9**. *We didn't cover that one in this book — what do you do?*

   1. *Relax and take a deep breath.*

   2. *Play a* **C♯7** *chord. (You definitely know that one.)*

   3. *Add a 9th but lower it one half-step — "flat" it.*

Chord symbols literally tell *you exactly what to do. Do it right, and you get the following chord:*

 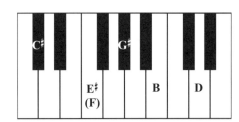

You might see ♭**9**, ♯**11**, ♭**6**, **add2**, *or others. Just do what it tells you...unless it says* **C♯-go-jump-off-a-cliff**. *(You can make that decision on your own.)*

Build the chord on a scale

You may not know the chord for **D7♯5(♭9)**, *but you know the root note* **(D)**. *Quickly make a major scale (see Appendix B) on this root note and find the notes you need. In other words, from what you've learned already, you should know that...*

   If there's an "m" in the chord symbol, you need a minor third above the root.

   If there's a "7" in the chord symbol, you'll need the seventh scale tone.

   If there's a "sus" in the chord symbol, you'll need a second or fourth in place of the third.

   If there's a "6," you'll need the sixth scale tone.

   and so on, and so on...

Once you have all of your necessary notes, make the alterations described in the chord symbol, such as ♯**13**, ♭**5**, **(no 3rd)**, **maj7**, **add9**, *or whatever. The illustration below shows how this is done for a* **D7♯5(♭9)** *chord.*

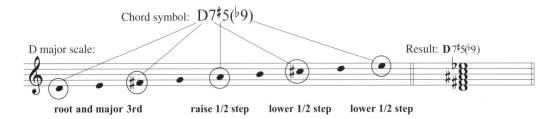

Use a numeric recipe

This idea is similar to building a chord on a scale. But this time you have the aid of a chart. (Gotta like that!) Find the correct root note and make a major scale from it. Then, look up the funky chord symbol on the following chart and add the scale tones indicated by the numeric recipe.

Chord Symbol	Chord Type	Scale Tones
C	major	1-3-5
Cm	minor	1-♭3-5
C+	augmented	1-3-♯5
Cdim	diminished	1-♭3-♭5
Csus, Csus4	suspended fourth	1-4-5
Csus2	suspended second	1-2-5
C6	added sixth	1-3-5-6
Cm6	minor, added sixth	1-♭3-5-6
C7	dominant seventh	1-3-5-♭7
Cmaj7	major seventh	1-3-5-7
Cm7	minor seventh	1-♭3-5-♭7
Cdim7	diminished seventh	1-♭3-♭5-♭♭7 (6)
C7♯5	dominant seventh, raised fifth	1-3-♯5-♭7
Cm7♭5	minor seventh, lowered fifth	1-♭3-♭5-♭7
C(add9), C(add2)	added ninth (or added second)	1-3-5-9, or 1-2-3-5
C9	ninth	1-3-5-♭7-9
Cmaj9	major ninth	1-3-5-7-9
Cm9	minor ninth	1-♭3-5-♭7-9
C11	eleventh	1-3-5-♭7-9-11
C13	thirteenth	1-3-5-♭7-9-13

Ornaments aren't just for holidays anymore

An easy way to make your own style is by adding some "ornamentations" to the melody notes. (For you music theory buffs, these are really called *articulations*.) Following is a list of some of the more common ones and an explanation of what they mean.

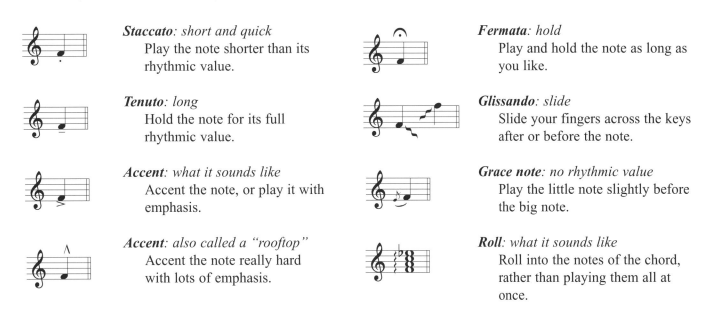

Staccato: *short and quick*
Play the note shorter than its rhythmic value.

Tenuto: *long*
Hold the note for its full rhythmic value.

Accent: *what it sounds like*
Accent the note, or play it with emphasis.

Accent: *also called a "rooftop"*
Accent the note really hard with lots of emphasis.

Fermata: *hold*
Play and hold the note as long as you like.

Glissando: *slide*
Slide your fingers across the keys after or before the note.

Grace note: *no rhythmic value*
Play the little note slightly before the big note.

Roll: *what it sounds like*
Roll into the notes of the chord, rather than playing them all at once.

Experiment and find the ones you like. Then pencil them onto any song you want to play. Ever heard "Kum-bah-yah" played in a short, snappy, staccato style? Me neither, but be my guest.

Try playing "Hot Time in the Old Town Tonight" with some of your new note ornamentations.

Hot Time in the Old Town Tonight

Words by Joe Hayden
Music by Theodore H. Metz

Five easy steps to faking a better arrangement

When you have all the chord-building, rhythmic-varying, melody-making tools under your belt, and you're ready to play a favorite song from a fake book, here are five quick steps you should do before playing a single note.

Doing this will help you survey the song and allows you to leave yourself little "reminder notes" about the type of accompaniment you want to play. Of course, with time and practice, you won't have to do this *every* time you play — it'll become second nature to you.

Step 1: Survey the chords

Take a quick look at every chord symbol in the song. Circle ones you don't know or may need to practice first. Also, be sure to consider which positions and inversions would be the best for smoother chord changes and pencil these in above the chord symbols.

Step 2: Simplify those complex chords

You don't feel like revoicing chords today? No problem — just reduce the bigger, more complex chords to smaller ones with similar scale tones (as described in Chapter 11). But remember to pencil your changes onto the music, so you won't have to think about scale-tone reductions while the barflies are listening.

Step 3: Dress up the melody

Pull out that list of articulations and ornamentations on page 72 and write in the ones you enjoy playing. Perhaps a few grace notes, a fermata, a quick glissando? Make the melody a style of your own.

Don't forget about rhythmic variations (covered back in Chapter 6). Syncopating the melody can really add a nice personal touch. Write in rhythm changes on the music, so you won't forget.

Step 4: Creative bass lines

Think about where you want to hold chords, where you want quarter-note chords, an arpeggio or root-fifth bass, even a walking bass line. Don't make these decisions "on the fly" — pencil your ideas onto the music. Some piano players like to change the bass line pattern in each verse and chorus; others like to keep a consistent pattern going throughout.

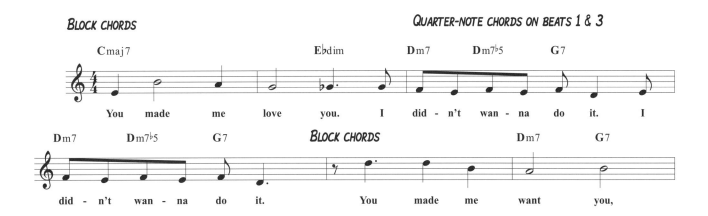

Step 5: Emphasize the rhythm

If you've tinkered with the melody rhythm, are you going to match this syncopation with your left hand chords or patterns? You can pencil in a rhythmic figure over the first bar to show what chord rhythm to play throughout.

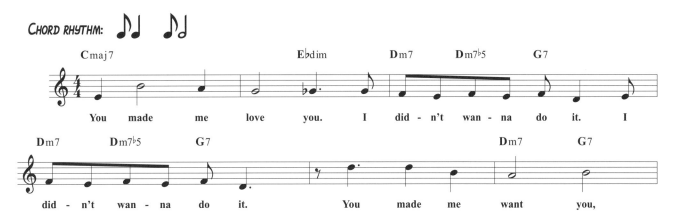

It may seem like a lot of effort for playing a few short songs, but it really doesn't take that much time. And the results will be well worth the wait.

Take a breath, filter all of this through your brain one last time, turn the page and get ready to play two final songs.

Put it all together

Apply the five-step process to these two final songs. Try both of them several times, several ways, with different musical ideas each time. (This is why we use *pencil*, not indelible markers!)

You Made Me Love You

Words by Joseph McCarthy
Music by Jimmy Monaco

Look for the Silver Lining

Words by B.G. DeSylva
Music by Jerome Kern

Now treat yourself for a job well done…go buy some fake books.

APPENDIX A
Chord recipes

When all else fails, look it up — right here! The information on this page should help you create all of the chords covered in this book. Just find the chord and play the notes given. (Enharmonics have been simplified.)

C chords

C	C-E-G
Cm	C-E♭-G
Cdim	C-E♭-G♭
C+	C-E-G♯
Csus	C-F-G
C6	C-E-G-A
Cm6	C-E♭-G-A
C7	C-E-G-B♭
Cmaj7	C-E-G-B
Cm7	C-E♭-G-B♭
Cdim7	C-E♭-G♭-A
C(add9)	C-E-G-D
C9	C-E-G-B♭-D
Cmaj9	C-E-G-B-D
Cm9	C-E♭-G-B♭-D
C11	C-E-G-B♭-D-F
C13	C-E-G-B♭-D-A

C♯ or D♭ chords

C♯	C♯-F-G♯
C♯m	C♯-E-G♯
C♯dim	C♯-E-G
C♯+	C♯-F-A
C♯sus	C♯-F♯-G♯
C♯6	C♯-F-G♯-A♯
C♯m6	C♯-E-G♯-A♯
C♯7	C♯-F-G♯-B
C♯maj7	C♯-F-G♯-C
C♯m7	C♯-E-G♯-B
C♯dim7	C♯-E-G-B♭
C♯(add9)	C♯-D♯-F-G♯
C♯9	C♯-F-G♯-B-D♯
C♯maj9	C♯-F-G♯-C-D♯
C♯m9	C♯-E-G♯-B-D♯
C♯11	C♯-F-G♯-B-D♯-F♯
C♯13	C♯-F-G♯-B-D♯-A♯

D chords

D	D-F♯-A
Dm	D-F-A
Ddim	D-F-A♭
D+	D-F♯-A♯
Dsus	D-G-A
D6	D-F♯-A-B
Dm6	D-F-A-B
D7	D-F♯-A-C
Dmaj7	D-F♯-A-C♯
Dm7	D-F-A-C
Ddim7	D-F-A♭-B
D(add9)	D-E-F♯-A
D9	D-F♯-A-C-E
Dmaj9	D-F♯-A-C♯-E
Dm9	D-F-A-C-E
D11	D-F♯-A-C-E-G
D13	D-F♯-A-C-E-B

E♭ chords

E♭	E♭-G-B♭
E♭m	E♭-G♭-B♭
E♭dim	E♭-G♭-A
E♭+	E♭-G-B
E♭sus	E♭-A♭-B♭
E♭6	E♭-G-B♭-C
E♭m6	E♭-G♭-B♭-C
E♭7	E♭-G-B♭-D♭
E♭maj7	E♭-G-B♭-D
E♭m7	E♭-G♭-B♭-D♭
E♭dim7	E♭-G♭-A-C
E♭(add9)	E♭-F-G-B♭
E♭9	E♭-G-B♭-D♭-F
E♭maj9	E♭-G-B♭-D-F
E♭m9	E♭-G♭-B♭-D♭-F
E♭11	E♭-G-B♭-D♭-F-A♭
E♭13	E♭-G-B♭-D♭-F-C

E chords

E	E-G♯-B
Em	E-G-B
Edim	E-G-B♭
E+	E-G♯-C
Esus	E-A-B
E6	E-G♯-B-C♯
Em6	E-G-B-C♯
E7	E-G♯-B-D
Emaj7	E-G♯-B-D♯
Em7	E-G-B-D
Edim7	E-G-B♭-D♭
E(add9)	E-F♯-G♯-B
E9	E-G♯-B-D-F♯
Emaj9	E-G♯-B-D♯-F♯
Em9	E-G-B-D-F♯
E11	E-G♯-B-D-F♯-A
E13	E-G♯-B-D-F♯-C♯

F chords

F	F-A-C
Fm	F-A♭-C
Fdim	F-A♭-B
F+	F-A-C♯
Fsus	F-B♭-C
F6	F-A-C-D
Fm6	F-A♭-C-D
F7	F-A-C-E♭
Fmaj7	F-A-C-E
Fm7	F-A♭-C-E♭
Fdim7	F-A♭-B-D
F(add9)	F-G-A-C
F9	F-A-C-E♭-G
Fmaj9	F-A-C-E-G
Fm9	F-A♭-C-E♭-G
F11	F-A-C-E♭-G-B♭
F13	F-A-C-E♭-G-D

F♯ or G♭ chords

F♯	F♯-A♯-C♯
F♯m	F♯-A-C♯
F♯dim	F♯-A-C
F♯+	F♯-A♯-D
F♯sus	F♯-B-C♯
F♯6	F♯-A♯-C♯-D♯
F♯m6	F♯-A-C♯-D♯
F♯7	F♯-A♯-C♯-E
F♯maj7	F♯-A♯-C♯-F
F♯m7	F♯-A-C♯-E
F♯dim7	F♯-A-C-E♭
F♯(add9)	F♯-G♯-A♯-C♯
F♯9	F♯-A♯-C♯-E-G♯
F♯maj9	F♯-A♯-C♯-F-G♯
F♯m9	F♯-A-C♯-E-G♯
F♯11	F♯-A♯-C♯-E-G♯-B
F♯13	F♯-A♯-C♯-E-G♯-D♯

A chords

A	A-C♯-E
Am	A-C-E
Adim	A-C-E♭
A+	A-C♯-F
Asus	A-D-E
A6	A-C♯-E-F♯
Am6	A-C-E-F♯
A7	A-C♯-E-G
Amaj7	A-C♯-E-G♯
Am7	A-C-E-G
Adim7	A-C-E♭-F♯
A(add9)	A-B-C♯-E
A9	A-C♯-E-G-B
Amaj9	A-C♯-E-G♯-B
Am9	A-C-E-G-B
A11	A-C♯-E-G-B-D
A13	A-C♯-E-G-B-F♯

G chords

G	G-B-D
Gm	G-B♭-D
Gdim	G-B♭-D♭
G+	G-B-D♯
Gsus	G-C-D
G6	G-B-D-E
Gm6	G-B♭-D-E
G7	G-B-D-F
Gmaj7	G-B-D-F♯
Gm7	G-B♭-D-F
Gdim7	G-B♭-D♭-E
G(add9)	G-A-B-D
G9	G-B-D-F-A
Gmaj9	G-B-D-F♯-A
Gm9	G-B♭-D-F-A
G11	G-B-D-F-A-C
G13	G-B-D-F-A-E

B♭ chords

B♭	B♭-D-F
B♭m	B♭-D♭-F
B♭dim	B♭-D♭-E
B♭+	B♭-D-F♯
B♭sus	B♭-E♭-F
B♭6	B♭-D-F-G
B♭m6	B♭-D♭-F-G
B♭7	B♭-D-F-A♭
B♭maj7	B♭-D-F-A
B♭m7	B♭-D♭-F-A♭
B♭dim7	B♭-D♭-E-G
B♭(add9)	B♭-C-D-F
B♭9	B♭-D-F-A♭-C
B♭maj9	B♭-D-F-A-C
B♭m9	B♭-D♭-F-A♭-C
B♭11	B♭-D-F-A♭-C-E♭
B♭13	B♭-D-F-A♭-C-G

G♯ or A♭ chords

A♭	A♭-C-E♭
A♭m	A♭-B-E♭
A♭dim	A♭-B-D
A♭+	A♭-C-E
A♭sus	A♭-D♭-E♭
A♭6	A♭-C-E♭-F
A♭m6	A♭-B-E♭-F
A♭7	A♭-C-E♭-G♭
A♭maj7	A♭-C-E♭-G
A♭m7	A♭-B-E♭-G♭
A♭dim7	A♭-B-D-F
A♭(add9)	A♭-B♭-C-E♭
A♭9	A♭-C-E♭-G♭-B♭
A♭maj9	A♭-C-E♭-G-B♭
A♭m9	A♭-B-E♭-G♭-B♭
A♭11	A♭-C-E♭-G♭-B♭-D♭
A♭13	A♭-C-E♭-G♭-B♭-F

B chords

B	B-D♯-F♯
Bm	B-D-F♯
Bdim	B-D-F
B+	B-D♯-G
Bsus	B-E-F♯
B6	B-D♯-F♯-G♯
Bm6	B-D-F♯-G♯
B7	B-D♯-F♯-A
Bmaj7	B-D♯-F♯-A♯
Bm7	B-D-F♯-A
Bdim7	B-D-F-A♭
B(add9)	B-C♯-D♯-F♯
B9	B-D♯-F♯-A-C♯
Bmaj9	B-D♯-F♯-A♯-C♯
Bm9	B-D-F♯-A-C♯
B11	B-D♯-F♯-A-C♯-E
B13	B-D♯-F♯-A-C♯-G♯

Remember, if you need a chord's enharmonic equivalent (like a **G♯** instead of an **A♭** chord), make the necessary changes to all of the enharmonic notes in the chord spelling.

APPENDIX B
Help with scales and keys

Major and minor scales and key signatures are extremely important to know. So, if you don't know 'em already, here's a nice cheat sheet.

The twelve major scales   **The twelve minor scales**

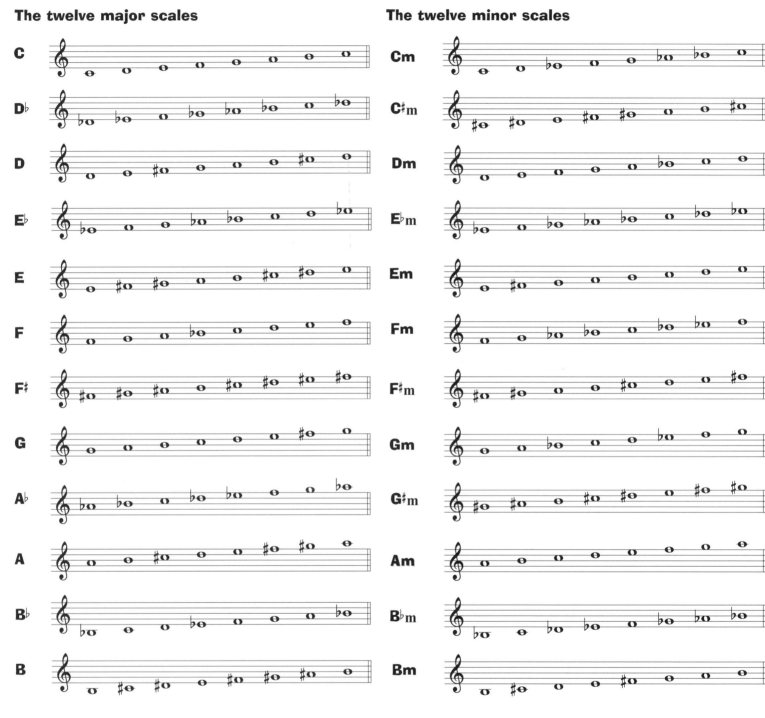

Key signatures you should know by heart

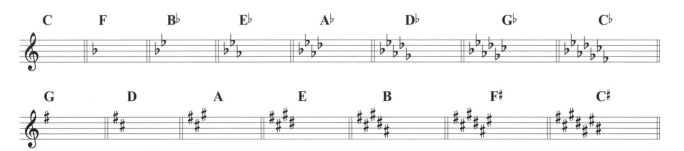

APPENDIX C:
Song index

A complete list of all the songs in this book — what a great thing to have! Maybe you want to impress your friends and relatives with that stylish tune full of major seventh chords. Perhaps you can't remember the lyrics to "Frankie and Johnny." Or you may just want to skip to a song you love.

Whatever the reason, you've got the whole list in your hands, you've got the whole long list in your hands…

THE ULTIMATE COLLECTION OF
FAKE BOOKS

The Ultimate Fake Book – 2nd Edition

Over 1200 songs, including: All I Ask of You • All the Things You Are • Always • And So It Goes • Autumn in New York • Blue Skies • Body and Soul • Call Me Irresponsible • Can't Help Falling in Love • Caravan • Easter Parade • Endless Love • Heart and Soul • The Impossible Dream • Isn't It Romantic? • The Lady Is a Tramp • Lay Down Sally • Let's Fall in Love • Moon River • My Funny Valentine • Piano Man • Roxanne • Satin Doll • Sophisticated Lady • Speak Low • Splish Splash • Strawberry Fields Forever • Tears in Heaven • A Time for Us (Love Theme from Romeo & Juliet) • Unforgettable • When I Fall in Love • When You Wish upon a Star • and hundreds more!

00240024 C Edition $45.00
00240025 E♭ Edition $45.00
00240026 B♭ Edition $45.00

Best Fake Book Ever - 2nd Edition

More than 1000 songs from all styles of music, including: All My Loving • American Pie • At the Hop • The Birth of the Blues • Cabaret • Can You Feel the Love Tonight • Don't Cry for Me Argentina • Dust in the Wind • Fever • Free Bird • From a Distance • The Girl from Ipanema • Hello, Dolly! • Hey Jude • I Heard It Through the Grapevine • The Keeper of the Stars • King of the Road • Longer • Misty • Route 66 • Sentimental Journey • Somebody • Somewhere in Time • Song Sung Blue • Spanish Eyes • Spinning Wheel • Take the "A" Train • Unchained Melody • We Will Rock You • What a Wonderful World • Wooly Bully • Y.M.C.A. • You're So Vain • and hundreds more.

00290239 C Edition $45.00
00240083 B♭ Edition $45.00
00240084 E♭ Edition $45.00

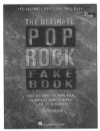

The Ultimate Pop/Rock Fake Book - 3rd Edition

Over 500 pop standards and contemporary hits, including: Addicted To Love • Ain't No Mountain High Enough • All Shook Up • Another One Bites The Dust • Can You Feel The Love Tonight • Crocodile Rock • Crying • Don't Know Much • Dust in the Wind • Earth Angel • Every Breath You Take • Have I Told You Lately • Hero • Hey Jude • Hold My Hand • Imagine • Layla • The Loco-Motion • Maggie May • Me and Bobby McGee • Mission: Impossible Theme • Oh, Pretty Woman • On Broadway • The Power of Love • Save the Best for Last • Spinning Wheel • Stand by Me • Stayin' Alive • Tears in Heaven • True Colors • The Twist • Vision Of Love • What's Going On • A Whole New World • Wild Thing • Wooly Bully • Yesterday • You've Lost That Lovin' Feelin' • and many more!

00240099 $35.00

The Ultimate Jazz Fake Book

Over 625 jazz classics spanning more than nine decades and representing all the styles of jazz. Includes: All of Me • All the Things You Are • Basin Street Blues • Birdland • Desafinado • A Foggy Day • I Concentrate on You • In the Mood • Take the "A" Train • Yardbird Suite • and many more!

00240079 C Edition $39.95
00240081 E♭ Edition $39.95
00240080 B♭ Edition $39.95

The Hal Leonard Real Jazz Book

A unique collection of jazz material in a wide variety of styles with no song duplication from The Ultimate Jazz Fake Book! Includes over 500 songs including a great deal of hard-to-find repertoire and a significant number of songs which have never before been printed.

00240097 C Edition $35.00
00240122 E♭ Edition $35.00
00240123 B♭ Edition $35.00

The Ultimate Broadway Fake Book - 4th Edition

More than 670 show-stoppers from over 200 shows! Includes: Ain't Misbehavin' • All I Ask of You • As If We Never Said Goodbye • Bewitched • Camelot • Memory • Don't Cry for Me Argentina • Edelweiss • I Dreamed a Dream • If I Were a Rich Man • Oklahoma • People • Seasons of Love • Send in the Clowns • Someone What I Did for Love • and more.

00240046 $39.95

The Classical Fake Book

An unprecedented, amazingly comprehensive reference of over 650 classical themes and melodies for all classical music lovers. Includes everything from Renaissance music to Vivaldi and Mozart to Mendelssohn. Lyrics in the original language are included when appropriate.

00240044 $24.95

The Beatles Fake Book

200 songs including: All My Loving • And I Love Her • Back in the USSR • Can't Buy Me Love • Day Tripper • Eight Days a Week • Eleanor Rigby • Help! • Here Comes the Sun • Hey Jude • Let It Be • Michelle • Penny Lane • Revolution • Yesterday • and many more.

00240069 $25.00

The Ultimate Country Fake Book

Over 700 super country hits, including: Achy Breaky Heart • Act Naturally • The Chair • Friends In Low Places • Grandpa (Tell Me 'Bout the Good Old Days) • Islands in the Stream • Jambalaya • Love Without End, Amen • No One Else on Earth • Okie From Muskogee • Stand By Me • and more.

00240049 $39.95

Wedding & Love Fake Book

Over 400 classic and contemporary songs, including: All for Love • All I Ask of You • Anniversary Song • Ave Maria • Can You Feel the Love Tonight • Endless Love • Forever and Ever, Amen • Forever in Love • I Wanna Be Loved • It Could Happen to You • Misty • Saving All My Love • So in Love • Through the Years • Vision of Love • and more.

00240041 $24.95

The Irving Berlin Fake Book

Over 150 Berlin songs, including: Alexander's Ragtime Band • Always • Blue Skies • Easter Parade • God Bless America • Happy Holiday • Heat Wave • I've Got My Love to Keep Me Warm • Puttin' on the Ritz • White Christmas • and more.

00240043 $19.95

The Ultimate Christmas Fake Book - 3rd Edition

More than 200 holiday tunes, including traditional classics and contemporary favorites: Blue Christmas • The Chipmunk Song • Frosty the Snowman • I'll Be Home for Christmas • Silent Night • Silver Bells • and more!

00240045 $19.95

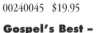

Gospel's Best – Words And Music

The best reference book of gospel music ever compiled! Here's a collection of over 500 of the greatest songs of our time, representing all areas of gospel music.

00240048 $24.95

FOR MORE INFORMATION, SEE YOUR LOCAL MUSIC DEALER, OR WRITE TO:

HAL•LEONARD®
CORPORATION

7777 W. BLUEMOUND RD. P.O. BOX 13819 MILWAUKEE, WI 53213
http://www.halleonard.com
Prices, contents and availability subject to change without notice